# RALPH'S ITALIAN RESTAURANT

## *100 Years and 100 Recipes*

8-RUBI

# RALPH'S ITALIAN RESTAURANT

*100 Years and 100 Recipes*

# Jimmy Rubino, Jr.
# with Ted Taylor

Library of Congress Number:          00-190870
ISBN #:          Hardcover          0-7388-2059-8
                 Softcover          0-7388-2060-1

**To order additional copies of this book, contact:**
Xlibris Corporation
1-888-7-XLIBRIS
www.Xlibris.com
Orders@Xlibris.com

# WELCOME . . .

The following recipes have been in my family for over 100 years, and have been passed down for four generations.

For the first time in the century that we have been in business, these guarded recipes have been written down. No one in my family has ever written down a recipe, including me, until now. After many hours of hard work and headaches, this is the outcome. I tried to keep it simple so anyone can cook from this book. (I wrote the recipes in capital letters so that this can be a functional cookbook, as well as a chronicle of the restaurant.) I hope you have as much fun creating these dishes as we do creating them for you at Ralph's!

Sincerely,
**Jimmy Rubino Jr.**

# CONTENTS

Ralph Dispigno at age 15

# FOREWORD

There are certain things I remember from my childhood that stand out as very special. Most of them are the places I would go with my father—the Boulevard at Broad and Oregon Avenue, the Colonial Theater at 11th and Moyamensing, the Lakes (League Island Park, where my dad, my brother John, and I would play baseball), George's Ice Cream Parlor for a great sundae, and of course, Ralph's Italian Restaurant at 9th and Catharine Streets. My dad and I had the greatest food there (and believe me, my dad was very particular about food—I guess that's where I got it). But Ralph's isn't only about food, it's a place where old friends meet, and where you can make new friends. The feeling is very much like a large family get-together, where everyone enjoys each other's company, and the very special food. I've never been to another restaurant quite like Ralph's.

Today when I go to Ralph's, the family feeling is exactly the same as it was when I was a kid. It's one of the very few things in this ever-changing world that I can truly say has remained unchanged (and thus, perfect). The wonderful feeling of being welcomed, the warmth and friendliness . . . and, a drum roll please—the FOOD!

Many a restaurant has one or two dishes that you particularly like, but at Ralph's, everything is incredible: the sausage and peppers; the potatoes and onions are beyond compare; the grilled veal chop is out of this world; the numerous pasta dishes are distinctive, rich, and wonderful; the chicken and veal specials are delicate and savory; the delectable salads and antipasto (man, am I getting hungry!)—and most of all, that immensely special feeling that you are eating in the warmth, comfort, and serenity of your own home.

I could go on and on, but the one last thing I'll say is this: every time I come to Philly, my very first stop is Ralph's Italian Restaurant. There, I share memorable food with old friends and new acquaintances, and what a special feeling it is.

When I think of Philadelphia, I can't help but think of Ralph's.

**James Darren**
**Beverly Hills, CA.**

James Darren whipping up some pasta in Ralph's kitchen.

# MY DESTINY . . .

## *A Lesson About Life*

At a very young age, I remember being in the restaurant, watching the hustle and bustle of everyone, and saying to myself, "This is what I want to do for the rest of my life." I recall seeing my grandfather, Ralph, orchestrate every move like a symphony, the waiters trying to serve their tables in a timely fashion, the chefs creating dishes—speaking broken English—the busboys making sure their tables had bread, water, and so on.

After years of hounding my Mother to get me a busboy uniform, my Grandfather finally said, "Elaine, its time." I remember the joy and excitement like it was yesterday. My brother, Eddie, who is four years older than me, was already working in the restaurant, so at six years old I was on my way—red velvet vest and all.

Learning to bus tables was my first order of business. This was just "buying time" until I was old enough to do what I really wanted to do—learn how to cook! Every chance I got, I spent in the kitchen watching and learning. (That was, of course, when the cooks would let me.)

I remember my Grandfather telling Eddie and me to stay out of the kitchen. "Cooking is hard enough without having two little boys in the way," he said. But that didn't stop me, and I think after a time they started not to mind me, as long as I stayed out of the way. As time went by, they even let me sweep the floor or clean the counters when they were finished. What a thrill that was. I felt like I was part of the team. This process went on and by the time I was twelve, I knew how to cook.

I have memories of meeting famous people. Athletes, movie

stars, TV stars, and other celebrities. Their presence at the restaurant was so commonplace that I was never "star struck." My friends were amazed at how little fuss I made about meeting all those famous people.

Fast-forward now twenty-five-years.

I sat down to write this book and realized that no one in my family had ever written a recipe down. When you were taught at Ralph's, you were "shown" how to do it, not given a piece of paper with ingredients written down. That method assured that no one would misinterpret the recipes. This has endured for 100 years, which to many of you might seem amazing.

There are actually lots of amazing things about Ralph's, so we have made this "more than a cookbook." Lots of things happen in a century, and Ralph's has been here for all of them. We decided to commemorate our 100th year with his book. With the help of James Darren, who has been like family to all of us for years, and my friend, Ted Taylor, we have created a book that we think will entertain and enlighten you. Ted has done a lot of the research on the history and evolution of the restaurant, and I have spent countless hours at the computer committing recipes and recollections to paper.

The prospect of having to put 100 recipes down on paper for this book was a little frightening at first. I just couldn't write ". . . put a little of this, a little of that . . . " so I had to start from scratch. But after months of writing, here we are.

The following recipes are the exact ingredients and method that we use to cook at Ralph's. I've tried to simplify each one as best I could. Cooking should be fun, not intimidating.

If you find a dish that needs more or less of say, salt, by all means express yourself and customize the recipe to your tastes and the way you want it. That's what cooking is all about. So, put on your apron and go have fun.

**Jimmy Rubino, Jr.**
**Philadelphia, PA.**

# PROLOGUE . . .

## *One American Institution Meets Another*

On Saturday, June 16, 1900, Theodore Roosevelt, the Governor of New York, and Thomas C. Platt, a Senator from the same state, arrived at North Philadelphia Station and made their way to the Walton Hotel in Center City.

The Governor was there reluctantly. While he aspired to the presidency at some point in his life—most likely 1904—he was in town because the Republican National Committee had pressured him to be there. Party leaders wanted him to be nominated as William McKinley's running mate at the GOP Convention. The gathering was to begin on Tuesday, June 19.

A Harvard graduate, the hero of the Spanish-American War where he served as Colonel of the famed "Rough Riders," a former New York City Police commissioner, former Under Secretary of the Navy, and one-time cowboy, he was the stuff of legends.

He was a man of the people—a heroic, stocky figure with a wild mustache, toothy smile, and trademark glasses. He was as happy with a group of laborers as he was with the cream of the country's high society.

As the story has been handed down over the years, T. R. was under siege in his Walton Hotel suite from the first light of dawn on Sunday. First, one state delegation would descend on him and then, another. Each group told him the same story. With Teddy as McKinley's running mate, the GOP would win and carry the local candidates with him from coast-to-coast, without him, they had no chance.

Roosevelt, according to history, would greet each delegation, flash his famous smile and tell them that he wasn't interested. Outside the hotel, a local Philadelphia character named "Buttons" Bimberg was already hawking McKinley-Roosevelt campaign buttons.

It was sometime on Tuesday, June 19, that Roosevelt, accompanied by Senator Platt's son Frank, went for a walk in Center City to clear his head and weigh his options. A meeting was scheduled by the New York delegation, of which Roosevelt was an at-large member. He wanted to think through the implications of a run for the vice presidency.

It wasn't long into his walk before Roosevelt had worked up an appetite—he was noted for his appreciation of good food—and ended up in a small restaurant that had been recently opened by Francesco and Catherine Dispigno.

He was in an environment he loved—among the people. The "backbone of America," he called them. Most of the hard working people of the enclave in the vicinity of 9th & Catherine Streets probably didn't even know who he was. But whomever he was—this stout man with the military bearing—they knew that he cut quite a figure. Wearing his black, wide-brimmed, felt hat—looking much like the one he wore as head of the Rough Riders—he was set apart from the locals as he made his way in to the Dispigno's establishment and ordered something to eat.

Time has forgotten what it was. Could it have been spaghetti, Calamari, or Lasagna? Did he drink a beer? Maybe a glass of red wine? It's really not important. What is important is that he liked it, and as legend recalls, heartily thanked the Dispignos for their service. He paid for his food, and as he departed, likely uttered his trademark phrase of praise, "Bully."

History does tell us what happened next.

That night at the New York delegation, he accepted a nomination for the vice presidency. The next day, he strode in to Convention Hall in West Philadelphia wearing that same black felt hat. It was then that insiders knew he was their man. On Thursday, following lunch with General Francis V. Greene, Teddy delivered a highly charged address seconding the presidential nomination for William McKinley.

The names of all other candidates for Vice President were withdrawn and Roosevelt was unanimously picked to be McKinley's running mate. The band struck up the Spanish-American War tune "There'll be A Hot Time in the Old Town Tonight" as the nomination was announced.

On March 4, 1901, in a heavy rainstorm, McKinley and Roosevelt were sworn in. The next day, Roosevelt presided over his first session of the U. S. Senate, which had been specially convened by the President to deal with presidential appointments.

On Friday, September 6, 1901, President McKinley was in Buffalo, NY, to preside over the Pan American Exposition. He was greeting well-wishers when a demented anarchist named Leon Czolgosz fired two shots into him at point blank range.

McKinley took one shot in the chest, the other in his abdomen. Roosevelt rushed to Buffalo to be by his side. At first, it appeared that McKinley had suffered only minor wounds and would surely recover, so Roosevelt returned home. But on the following Friday, which happened to be the 13th, McKinley's improving condition reversed. He passed away the next day. Roosevelt arrived in Buffalo shortly after McKinley's death and was sworn in as the 26th President of the United States.

Roosevelt was elected to the presidency again in 1904, but opted not to seek a third term. He designated William Howard Taft as his successor instead. For the next two years, he toured Europe and Africa.

In 1910, he returned to the campaign trail and traveled the country on behalf of various GOP candidates. It was at that point that he decided to make another run for the presidency, but failed to gain the Republican nomination in 1912. His run for the office as candidate of the third-party (Progressive) "Bull Moose" ticket cost Taft his re-election and allowed Woodrow Wilson to capture the White House.

In 1914, he led the campaign for U. S. preparedness in intervention on the Allied side, after war broke out in Germany. Two years later, the Progressive Party asked him to run again, but he declined and campaigned for GOP standard-bearer Charles Evans Hughes.

In 1917, at age 58, he asked President Wilson if he could lead a volunteer division of soldiers in World War I. He was refused, and the youngest of his four sons died in that war.

In 1918, he declined a bid to run for Governor of New York and, late in the year, was hospitalized with inflammatory rheumatism. On January 6, 1919, he died in his sleep at his home in Sagamore Hill, NY. He was 60 years old.

Almost a century after his political detractors called him, "That damn Cowboy," Roosevelt is acknowledged as one of the greatest presidents who ever resided in the White House.

It is ironic that exactly 100 years after Ralph's Restaurant was founded, the GOP met in Philadelphia, and the legendary "T.R." dined there, the Republican National Convention returned to the city and the spirit of Teddy Roosevelt lived on, as Ralph's began its second century.

### Bully for Teddy Roosevelt and Bully for Ralph's . . .

—by Ted Taylor

**Note:** Sources for this prologue include the *Encyclopedia Britannica,* the book *Departing Glory* by *Joseph L. Gardner (1973)* and The Theodore Roosevelt Association, Oyster Bay, NY, John A. Gable, PhD, executive director.

# The Oldest Family-Owned Italian Restaurants In America

1. *RALPH'S ITALIAN RESTAURANT, (The Dispigno Family) Phila., Pa., Founded 1900*

2. *BARBETTA'S, (The Miaellia Family) New York City, NY, Founded 1906*

3. *DANTE & LUIGI'S, (The DiRocco Family\*) Phila., Pa., Founded 1907*

4. *JEVELLI'S RESTAURANT, (The Jevelli Family) Boston, Mass., Founded 1924*

5. *THE COMO INN, (The Marchetti Family) Chicago, Ill., Founded 1924*

*\*The DiRocco family no longer owns and operates this restaurant.*

**Sources:** Research On Demand, Berkeley, CA. (search #91-7-15) commissioned by the owners of Fior D'Italia; The Chicago Tribune, Chicago Sun Times, Boston Globe, New York Daily News, Gourmet Magazine (NYC), and The Philadelphia Inquirer.

**Notes:** *Fior D'Italia*, located in San Francisco (North Beach area), was founded in 1886 but has had multiple ownership changes since it was opened. It is the oldest Italian Restaurant in America. The *Union Oyster House* in Boston has been owned by Italian families since it opened in 1826 (currently by the Milano Family) but does not advertise itself as an Italian specialty restaurant.

# CHAPTER ONE

## *The Dispignos Discover Philadelphia*

It was 1893 when Francesco and Catherine Dispigno, and their little boy Ralph, arrived at Ellis Island from Naples, Italy. Like many others, they believed that this country was a place where they could make a good life for themselves and pursue the fabled "American Dream."

The Dispignos knew that the only way to be successful was hard work, and they weren't afraid of that. Leaving New York, they made their way to Philadelphia and settled down in an Italian enclave around 9th and Catharine Sts., where they began to fashion their dream.

At the dawn of the 20th Century, South Philadelphia was exploding. There were Italians, Jews, Poles, Blacks, and Irishmen living there. Francesco's neighborhood was made up of hard workers—men and women who toiled from sunrise to sunset at backbreaking jobs. Often, they went home virtually too tired to eat.

The population of South Philadelphia during this time was 282,000—an increase of 60,000 in a decade. Of that population, only 14,540 were Italian, like the Dispignos. The Irish were still the dominant ethnic group, though the Italians were quickly closing the gap.

Multiple-family residences were the norm in that part of the city. Often, entire families shared one room. Their toilets were outside and often shared with their neighbors.

Francesco had a vision. He felt that his neighbors would appreciate a place where they could go and get a good meal and some refreshment. As a family man with a 10-year-old son, he believed in his heart that his neighborhood was the right place for a small restaurant and so he gathered all his savings and took a chance.

The Dispignos, having come from a region that offered Italy's best cooking, had quite an advantage. They knew and understood the Italian cuisine. It was from there that the world learned of pizza, sausage, and spaghetti. Of macaroni with clam, meat, tomato, or garlic sauces. All staples then, all staples today.

The Italian Market sprung up in an area that had once been the domain of the Irish. It wasn't yet called the Italian Market, but Sicilian and Southern Italian merchants began to sell everything from live chickens to fruits and vegetables. Soon they were joined by the Jews, who added the dimension of dry goods and clothing. The area became a magnet for shoppers from all over the city.

Francesco's vision led him to a building at 901 Montrose Street, in the midst of this burgeoning marketplace, which he rented, and soon opened his restaurant. The Dispigno family worked hard at their new business. The restaurant meant long, long hours and lots of hard work, but they were equal to the challenge.

In 1905, their son Ralph, now 15, was forced to leave school and work full-time in the family business, the restaurant. It was at this point that Francesco realized his restaurant was destined to be a long-term family business, and he purchased the Montrose Street building outright. As much of a visionary as Francesco was however, it is doubtful that he ever dreamed that one day, his restaurant would be America's oldest family-owned Italian restaurant. Which, of course, it is today. (1.)

Over the next decade the restaurant grew and prospered, and in 1915, the Dispignos made a major decision. Their business had simply outgrown the Montrose Street location. The Dispignos, now among the area's most prosperous business people, searched South Philadelphia for a bigger place and found a boarding house, built in the late 1800's at 760 South 9th Street, that fit the bill. They purchased the boarding house – and another house on the same block, where Francesco and Catherine would reside – and moved the business to where it stands today.

Without missing a beat, they converted the first two floors to dining space, installed a fashionable wood bar, and continued their 15-year tradition of serving Italian food to their South Philly neighbors.

In reality though, they served more than their neighbors. Because of the location near the market, merchants from all over the tri-State area converged daily on 9th Street and began to sample the excellent food at the restaurant – and their reputation spread.

The harbor of Francesco's homeland, an island off Naples

Ralph's Founder, Francesco Dispigno

# THE BATON IS PASSED TO RALPH

Ralph loved the business and was an apt pupil. His father, Francesco, taught him well. The restaurant flourished and Ralph became one of the leading businessmen in South Philadelphia. He used the bedrooms on the third floor of his building as a small hotel and it served as a first home in the New World for several of his immigrant cooks and waiters. He was, in fact, the Padrone of many immigrants. Francesco passed away in the early 1930's, but by then, Ralph was in complete charge of the day-to-day operation.

Ralph Dispigno Jr., Ralph's oldest son—who still makes his presence felt at the restaurant—recalls that the rooms were still being occupied by Italian immigrants well into the late 1940's. "My Father would sponsor people who wanted to come to this country," Ralph recalled, "and they would live up there on the third floor until they got on their feet."


QUOTABLE . . .

". . . They come and they go. Some stay. Like for 100 years. Ralph's was founded in 1900 and still run by the same family . . ."
—Michael Klein, "Table Talk", The Philadelphia Inquirer, 8/15/99

Mary & Ralph Dispigno enjoy a bottle of fine wine.

Ralph sits at the first floor bar circa 1930's.
Note the tile floor, still in use at Ralph's.

# CHAPTER TWO

## *Growing Up In A Restaurant*

The restaurant business was a family business, and Ralph Sr. had six children: Frank, Catherine, Ralph Jr., Eleanor, Michael, and Elaine. Today, Elaine Dodaro, the youngest of Ralph's children, serves as president and treasurer of the restaurant. Her son, Jimmy Rubino Jr., is the owner/operator and head chef. His brother Eddie is an important member of the management team. Together, they represent the fourth generation of family ownership.

Ralph Jr. was born in 1929, unfortunately just in time to see his 39-year-old father lose virtually everything he owned in the stock market crash. Everything, that is, except the family business. "My father owned property all over South Philadelphia. When the market crashed he lost it all, everything but his restaurant. I remember hearing stories about how my parents (Ralph and Mary) sold bowls of spaghetti and meatballs out the front door for five cents just to keep a roof over our heads," Ralph said.

The depression and prohibition would have been enough to wipe out a less hearty family, but not the Dispignos. They kept working, kept offering the same quality of food and service that they always had, and their city-wide customer base responded with their support and kept them going.

George Chaby, a lifelong customer and president of Chaby International Umbrellas, recently told Ralph's general manager Ronnie Trombino that he recalled the days when Ralph would serve wine to his "good customers" in coffee cups. "It was done all the time during Prohibition, of course," Chaby recalled, "but it made you feel special."

The family has always been a big part of the business, and as Ralph and Mary's kids grew, they took their jobs seriously. Ralph Jr. learned to be an excellent chef. Michael and Eleanor both tended bar and Elaine was a waitress. Both Ralph Jr. and Michael were promising musicians, but both sacrificed their musical careers for the restaurant. It was the family thing, and the right thing to do, Ralph Jr. said.

During World War II, when "manpower" was at a premium, Eleanor recalls how she would come in and clean the restaurant in the morning then move out into the kitchen, where she helped in any way she could.

Elaine remembers days that she'd be home with her two sons, when her father would come to the house and say "Honey, we need you at the restaurant," and she'd have no choice – or no second thoughts – about going there to help. "It would usually be that someone, a dishwasher maybe, a waiter, had called in sick and my Father was short-handed," she recalls.

Like his father before him, Ralph Dispigno was a pillar of the community. He was honored countless times for his civic involvement and served as president of the Madonna House in the St. Paul's Roman Catholic Parish—the religious center of the South Philadelphia Italian community—for eleven years.

Elaine laughs when she recalls that her father ran the annual St. Paul's charity banquet for many years. "People would come here to eat and before they left, my father had sold them a ticket to the banquet. It was always sold out," she recalls. On March 29, 1966, the Italian Government honored him when the title of "Cavaliere" was bestowed upon him.

## JIMMY STARTS WORK AT AGE FIVE

It was about this time that little Jimmy Rubino began to take an interest in the family business run by his beloved "Poppy." Jimmy was five years old when he started to "work" at the restaurant. "I was born for this business," he said, "never a day has gone by that I didn't view this restaurant, this business, as my destiny."

Jimmy was a serious five-year-old, and he told his Mom, Elaine, that he should be dressed just like all the other members of the restaurant staff. "In those days our waiters wore red jackets, white shirts, and black pants and I went crazy trying to find a red jacket for Jimmy," she recalls. One day, she was in center city Philadelphia shopping at Strawbridge and Clothier's and she spied a bright red kid's vest – it was perfect. Jimmy had his uniform.

And so, every Sunday, just like all the other waiters and staff members, little Jimmy would walk from his home – which happened to be next door – to the restaurant, carrying his "uniform" on a hanger. He would then go to the third floor and change like everyone else. It was the dawn of the fourth generation of family ownership.

By the time he was 13, Jimmy's Uncle Ralph had already taught him how to cook. Jimmy began as a busboy and then became a waiter, a job he held until he was 18 years old. It was then that he seriously turned his focus toward the kitchen.

Jimmy's brother Eddie also grew up in the business –and works in it today – but he left to pursue a career in the health care field and spent several years successfully pursuing that dream, working in home health care and as an emergency room nurse.

In a business where a five-year-run is the norm, Ralph's celebrates a landmark 100 years of consistently good food at the dawn of the new Millennium. This is a restaurant that has been in business through the terms of 19 American Presidents, that has survived two World Wars, a depression, prohibition, and countless local and national tragedies. It has been an oasis of fine dining for a century and has been honored countless times.

## QUOTABLE . . .

". . . Ralph's is the oldest family-owned Italian eatery in the country. It lays claim to being one of the favorite restaurants of many celebrities, including Tony Bennett and the late Frank Sinatra . . ." —Jennifer Kramer Williams, Restaurant Marketing Magazine, September/October 1999.

Jimmy at work in the kitchen

Eddie Rubino, Ralph Dispigno, Jr., Elaine Dodaro,
Jimmy Rubino, Jr.

# CHAPTER THREE

## *This Old House*

After almost 15 years at the Montrose Street location, the Dispigno's knew that if their business was going to grow, it would have to do so at a larger location. So, they began their search for a new location.

The three-story brownstone that houses Ralph's today was the place that Francesco and Catherine decided would be their new location. Built in the 1880's, the building would prove to be the foundation of the Ralph's legend.

A picture of Ralph's from the 1920's shows Ralph himself, holding court at the first floor bar, a striped awning overhead. A mirror behind the bartender reflects the room, while a large oak cash register perches at the end of the bar. (That original bar is on the second floor today, cut and shaped so that it will fit in the back of the dining room.) There were tables lined along the right side as you entered, and a huge mirror close by the stairway to the second floor and the doorway to the kitchen.

The second floor today looks pretty much as it always has— the large overhead lights and fans, the murals on the wall (copies of the original artwork that had been painted there), and the tin ceiling. In the back of the second floor, the original artwork remains on the walls. On the opposite wall is the Ralph's crest, a shield with "R R" on it. An ancient air conditioner, that Rubino says works as good as it did when it was installed in the 1950's, occupies a corner of the room near the steps.

The steps themselves are part of the Ralph's legend. They are narrow, befitting an old house, and there's a sharp turn before you hit the second floor.

Before it became a 40-seat dining room and private party room, as well as Ralph's executive offices and Rubino's private wine cellar (that is, really, a wine attic), the third floor was a hotel. It has been totally renovated, but the old brick walls still remain and Francesco's original winepress is on display there.

Since the building is well over 100 years old, there was no way to install "dumb waiters." As a consequence, when all three floors are full of diners—as is the case most evenings—Ralph's waiters carry full trays of food from the kitchen up three flights of narrow stairs.

When asked by a third-floor diner recently if they had "dumb waiters," long-time Ralph's staff member John "J. R." Paoloka said, "Yes, we all are," and then gave a hearty laugh.

You never think of it, but as you walk through the front door of Ralph's, you immediately find yourself standing on a work of art. Few people probably ever think of the floor at Ralph's as a work of art, but it truly is.

The tile floor was already in place in 1915, when the Dispignos bought the boarding house at 760 South 9th Street and moved the restaurant a couple of blocks from where it had been located since 1900.

"The tile work and design represents an art form and crafts-manship that has been lost in our modern times. We guess that the work was done in the 1890's," said Jimmy Rubino, Jr.

"Each tile on both the first and second floor was carefully put in place, one-at-a-time," he added, "In fact, if you look at the floors very closely, you can detect variations in the design where the artist perhaps was distracted, or quit for the day."

The irony of the story is that the tile work on the first floor was almost lost forever.

Back in 1972—a year after Ralph Dispigno, Sr., Francesco's son, had died—his children, now operating the restaurant, de-cided that it was time to modernize and renovate the place. Not only was the entrance re-done and the walls flocked, but a slate floor was placed over top of the tile and embedded in cement. "No one really thought of the tile as anything but an old floor then and the idea was to 'modernize' the place," Rubino, who was 11-at-the-time, said. And so, for 21 years, the tile on the first floor remained covered.

In 1993, it was time for another renovation and the family decided to have the slate floor removed and replaced with, of all things, a tile floor. "We picked the tile, bought it, hired a contractor and ordered the work to be done," Rubino recalled.

His mother, Elaine, the youngest of Ralph's children, and Ralph Jr., who were operating the restaurant at the time, decided to close for a couple of weeks that summer so that the renovations could go on without interruption.

"Everybody went away on vacation, except me," Rubino recalls, "and I'd stop by and see how the work was going every day. And one day I walked through the door and there were workmen with sledgehammers whacking away at the slate floor and as it came up, I noticed that the old tile was not only still intact, but it was undamaged and, frankly, very beautiful."

Rubino laughs when he recalls what happened next. "I saw the old floor and just as the guy was about to take another whack at it I dove in front of him, on my hands and knees, and yelled 'stop' as loud as I could. The guy thought I was nuts, but he stopped."

Almost like a miracle, the old floor was undamaged and preserved below the slate and cement and, on Rubino's orders, the rest of it was removed very carefully.

Jimmy decided that the old floor should be restored and instructed everyone not to tell Elaine and to keep it as a surprise for her when she returned from vacation. Elaine was in California visiting family friend James Darren, the actor/singer, and had no idea what was transpiring in South Philadelphia. She received no hint when she called to see "how things were going".

Over the next week or so, the workmen cleaned and polished

the old floor and, recalls Rubino, "We were stuck with a load of new tile that we had already purchased for the restaurant floor."

Elaine returned home after two weeks at 9 p.m. on a Sunday night, and arrived at her residence, which is next door to the restaurant. Jimmy met her and said that he had a surprise for her. "We made her close her eyes as she walked in to the restaurant," Jimmy said, "to build up the suspense."

"I didn't know what they were up to," Elaine recalls, "but I never expected to see the old floor shining and bright, just as I remembered it as a child. All I could say was 'Oh, My God', it was like a miracle."

A miracle that visitors to Ralph's can not only behold and enjoy—but walk on without fear of anything happening to it.

## QUOTABLE . . .

". . . Bully for Ralph's! Surely that's what Theodore Roosevelt said a hundred years ago after enjoying dinner at Francesco and Catherine Dispigno's spiffy new restaurant in South Philadelphia's Italian market . . . but the proof of just how good Ralph's is, and why it promises to extend its proud history well into the 21$^{st}$ Century, lies with my own seventy-something Mother, Clara Quattrone, a lifelong South Philadelphia resident, who is one of the world's great Italian cooks. After her first dinner at Ralph's (in November, 1999), she repeated Teddy Roosevelt's approval—in her own distinctive way of course. Jimmy Rubino breathed a sigh of relief, laughed heartily, and invited her back. She said she'd be happy to return . . ."
—Frank D. Quattrone, Editor, Ticket Magazine, Montgomery Newspapers, November 24, 1999.

Front of Ralph's, 1970

The dining area at Ralph's in the 1930's.

# CHAPTER 4

## *A Celebrity Destination*

On February 27, 2000, well-known film and TV actor Vincent Schiavelli spent the day at Ralph's Restaurant meeting with customers and mingling with the staff. Schiavelli, known for his roles in such films as *Ghost* and *One Flew over the Cuckoos Nest*, as well as TV shows such as *Taxi* and *The X-Files*, is the Grandson of a Sicilian Chef and the author of three cookbooks. Vincent spent the day at Ralph's as part of the annual *Book and the Cook Celebration presented by Audi*.

Guests at Ralph's that Sunday could not only dine on traditional Ralph's fare, but also a special Sicilian Meatloaf dish from Schiavelli's cookbook, added to the menu for that day only.

Vincent fit in so well at Ralph's because of his Italian heritage and his genuine affection for good people and good food.

In a story that has been passed down from generation to generation, it is recalled that one hundred years ago, Theodore Roosevelt was a Ralph's Restaurant customer, and that's not so hard to believe. Roosevelt was also a man of the people, and it's easy to visualize old "Rough and Ready" sitting down to a hearty meal in the Italian Market at Ralph's. It's probably not even a stretch to consider that after he finished his meal, he said, "Bully for Ralph's."

When the Republican National Convention was held in Philadelphia in the summer of 2000, it had been exactly one hundred years since Teddy Roosevelt took to the rostrum at the 1900 Republican National Convention in Philadelphia, and seconded the nomination of William McKinley as the GOP standard bearer. One day later, history recalls, Roosevelt was unanimously selected as McKinley's running mate. It was also exactly one hundred years since Francesco Dispigno opened his landmark Italian restaurant in the City of Philadelphia.

President Roosevelt started something. He was the first of a long line of celebrities who found Ralph's warmth and hospitality to be a perfect fit. In the Frank Sinatra biography *The Way You Wear Your Hat*, author Bill Zahme identifies Ralph's as one of the singer's favorite Philadelphia eating places, and the Dispigno family has fond recollections of the many times Sinatra frequented the restaurant over the years.

A legendary Martini drinker, Ralph's family members all recall seeing the popular crooner standing back in the first floor service bar area—out of sight of his legions of fans—with a cigarette in one hand and a Martini in the other.

Movie Star James Darren, who grew up a few blocks from Ralph's in South Philadelphia, says, "Whenever I come home to Philadelphia, I take a cab right from the airport to Ralph's. I eat and then I proceed to my hotel."

Darren grew up at 10th & Ritner Sts. and started eating at Ralph's as a child. "My family always came here for dinner," he said. Darren and the Dispigno brothers—Ralph Jr. and Michael— became fast boyhood friends.

"Ralph's is truly a world class gourmet restaurant in a neighborhood setting," Darren added, "their food is incredibly consistent. I have never had a bad meal and the food is never less than excellent."

While appearing on the TV show *Melrose Place*, Darren told fellow star Heather Locklear about Ralph's. Soon afterwards, her career took her to Philadelphia and she ate dinner there—"She loved it," he reported with a smile.

While he grew up with Ralph's children, Darren has nothing but accolades for Jimmy Rubino Jr., Ralph's grandson and the fourth generation owner/operator of the restaurant.

"Jimmy has taken Ralph's to the next level. He is a very sharp young man, a great restaurateur. He runs a tight ship and he's a perfectionist. I like that. Successful people are always perfectionists," Darren added.

Elaine, Rubino's mother and Ralph's youngest child, recalls the parade of celebrities that made Ralph's a favorite haunt over the years. She recites names like Tony Bennett, John Casavettes, Peter Falk, Peter Frampton, Billy Ocean, Jerry Vale, Ann Jillian, Louis Prima, Fred Dryer, Sergio Franci, Al Martino, Sammy Davis Jr., Pat Cooper, Michael Keaton, and laughs when she recalls the time that actress Lena Horne came to the restaurant and created absolute chaos. "There was such a crowd surrounding her when she got here that my father got caught in the middle of it. He wore glasses, and his glasses got knocked off and he almost got trampled trying to retrieve them."

Elaine smiles as she paints a mental picture of her very staid and proper father struggling to regain his glasses.

Singer Al Martino recalls his times at Ralph with great pleasure. "Ralph was always happy to see me walk into his restaurant," Martino recalled recently. "He would sit with me and we would talk about the great times in South Philadelphia. Whenever I performed at *Palumbo's*, I looked forward to a great dinner at Ralph's. I now live in Beverly Hills, California, and I will continue dining at Ralph's whenever I'm in Philadelphia."

"People come from all over to eat at Ralph's," Darren said. "Basically, it was peasant food that has now been elevated to a gourmet class. It's like eating in your home. There is a true family feel there—you are never rushed, they tell you to 'take your time' eating, it's something that never changes. If I'm in Philadelphia for six nights, I'll go to Ralph's for dinner at least four of them."

Darren, who frequently appears as a singer at the Atlantic City resorts, usually prevails upon one of his relatives to bring him a dinner from Ralph's before he goes on. "I like the food and it makes me feel 'at home', so that's why I do it," he said.

General Manager Ronnie Trombino recalls the night when Ann Jillian and her husband arrived for dinner. "I wasn't at the front desk when they arrived and something happened and they decided to leave. I was coming out of the kitchen and saw this couple—I had no idea who they were—turning and leaving. I asked the former employee what had happened and, apparently, he was not willing to seat them where they wanted to be.

"I walked out the door and saw them walking about a block down Ninth Street and finally caught up with them," Trombino said. "I said I didn't know what had happened to make them leave, but I asked if they would give us another chance to serve them. The woman smiled, shook her head 'yes' and we walked back to the restaurant. I still had no idea who it was, I just knew that she was a very beautiful woman," Trombino continued.

Once back in Ralph's, Trombino found them a table to their liking and they were seated. "I walked back into the kitchen and one of our waiters told me that I had just seated Ann Jillian. I couldn't believe it, but I had. Later, she raved about the meal, said it was one of the best she had ever had, and signed a wonderful picture for us," Ronnie added.

Jimmy Rubino recalls the day that Dom DeLuise showed up, unannounced.

"I was in the kitchen and one of the waiters came back and said, 'I think Dom DeLuise is out front.' I told him he was probably mistaken, but I walked out to see for sure, and then I did a really strange thing. I saw him, realized who he was, pointed at him and blurted out, 'It's you.' He smiled up at me, pointed back, and said 'It's you, too' and that broke the ice."

DeLuise, a gourmet cook in his own right, had heard about Ralph's Calamari and wanted to find out if it was as good as it was reputed to be. He sat, alone, in the restaurant, ate the Calamari, escarole, and a loaf of Italian bread and then got up and left. "He had walked down here from Center City," Rubino said, "and when he was done, he raved about the meal, thanked us, and then walked north, back toward center city, and disappeared."

Ralph Dispigno Jr. recalled that DeLuise was appearing in a play at the Walnut Street Theater and that it was mid-afternoon and he "Just showed up and we didn't get much work done while he was here."

Ralph Jr. also names other native South Philadelphians, like Frankie Avalon, Bobby Rydell, Jack Klugman, Hy Lit, and Jerry Blavat, who all have been regular customers. Jimmy Durante, who frequently appeared up the street at *Palumbo's,* would also stop by for an Italian meal after he'd get done performing.

"My friend Henry Diamond and I would not let a week go by without eating at Ralph's," South Philly native Jack Klugman recalls, "I remember that while waiting for the wonderful entrée, we would put olive oil and cheese on that wonderful bread and glom it down. We would laugh as though we had discovered something no one else knew about. They were wonderful times, and Henry and I always talk about those days," he added.

"I never walked in to Ralph's Restaurant without being greeted by warm, smiling faces, and I am talking about a time when I was not a 'celebrity'. It's always nice to feel welcome," Klugman said.

When asked if he had a recipe that he'd like to share with readers of this book, Klugman laughed and said, "I do have a recipe for tomato and basil sauce, but since it can't compare with Ralph's I refuse to embarrass myself."

Cardinal Bevilauqua, the leader of Philadelphia's Roman Catholic Church, has been a Ralph's customer. Connie Mack, who was manager of the American League's Philadelphia Athletics baseball team for fifty years, was also a regular Ralph's customer.

In fact, sports celebrities gravitate to the place. Such superstars as Yogi Berra, Jersey Joe Walcott, Rocky Marciano, Joey Giardello, Gene Tenace, Tom LaSorda, The Niekro Brothers (Phil and Joe), Jerome Brown, and Charles Barkley have all enjoyed meals at Ralph's. Ralph Jr. recalls the day that NFL stars Bob Waterfield and Elroy "Crazy Legs" Hirsch came to the restaurant. "It was probably 1950, and they looked like fighters, big and rough. They were both playing for the Los Angeles Rams at the time and they had played the Eagles over at Shibe Park. What I also remember about Waterfield was that he was then married to movie star Jane Russell, so he was a pretty big celebrity himself."

Current Philadelphia Flyers' stars Eric Lindros and John LeClair are regular customers, as is former Phillies manager (and now Atlanta Braves coach) Pat Corrales. "We always draw a lot of current players," Rubino said. "Phillies players come in regularly, as do hockey and football players."

Darren, who was recently at Ralph's for lunch, summed it up when he said, "Thank God Ralph's is still going strong. I can't count the years I've been going there and what the place and the family means to me."

\*     \*     \*

**Pat Cooper's recipe for "An Italian Sandwich"**
*Bread is the secret . . .* Put olive oil on bread first, add ripe red tomatoes, semi hot peppers, any cold cuts will do . . . drink one glass of good Italian wine . . . *CIAO . . .*
"Most people don't have a clue how to make a good sandwich—bread is the secret," Cooper, America's favorite Italian comedian, said.

## Quotable . . .

". . . Almost every journalist in the country is currently scurrying around for stories with turn-of-the-century angles, I hate to brag, but I don't think any local food writer is going to come up with one better than this. Would you believe that Ralph's, an authentic "red gravy" restaurant, where I ate for the first time 45-years-ago, is celebrating its' 100th anniversary? . . . In a business where one year can become a lifetime, Ralph's has endured the equivalent of a millennium . . . Ralph's has the unique honor of being the oldest family-owned Italian restaurant in the United States . . . Ralph's has been in business through the terms of 19 American Presidents . . . You really can't go wrong with any of the food at Ralph's . . ."
—Len Lear, The Chestnut Hill Local, January 6, 2000.

Ann Jillian

James Darren

JERRY BLAVAT

Jerry Blavat

To Michael and Ralph's I was raised on your great food! Your the Best!

**HY LIT** "Hyski"

Hy Lit

Jerry Vale

A good Day at Ralph's—Pictured (left to right) Eddie Rubino,
Ron Trombino, Actor Vincent Schiavelli, Jimmy Rubino, Jr., Ted
Taylor—Part of the Book and the Cook Celebration.

Sergio Franci and Eleanor Dispigno Montella

# CHAPTER FIVE

## *A Century of Stories*

One hundred years is a long time, and Ralph's was at the heart of South Philly for all those years. People met here, had their first dates here, some were engaged here, wedding parties were held, graduation parties—even a funeral.

In fact, the funeral and viewing that were held at Ralph's gained citywide attention. Throngs of people jammed 9$^{th}$ Street and stood in long lines to view a hero who was being laid to rest from the second floor of Ralph's Italian Restaurant, in 1940. **James Clark**, a Philadelphia Police detective and brother-in-law of Ralph Dispigno, died a hero's death while trying to rescue people when a building exploded. Off-duty one day, Detective Clark happened to come upon a building that was a raging inferno. He entered the building, rescued a child, and then returned to try and save the child's mother. But as he was attempting to do that, the building collapsed and he was killed.

Ninth Street was closed to traffic during the funeral and then Philadelphia's **Mayor Lamberton** led the funeral procession from Ralph's to the cemetery, following the services.

\*     \*     \*

On a lighter note—but still concerning Detective Clark—during prohibition, Ralph's, like many Philadelphia restaurants, made and kept wine in the basement for special customers. Once, Clark called his brother-in-law to alert him of a possible police raid during which they would smash the bottles (just like we all saw on TV's "The Untouchables").

To be safe, Ralph himself emptied the contents of four full barrels so that no wine would be found on his premises. Having done that, he would avoid any problems when the police arrived.

The biggest problem was, however, the police *never* came! Whoops.

*     *     *

Being a chef at Ralph's takes a certain type of cat, because family tradition has it that they either prepare food in the "family style", or they are gone. First Francesco, then Ralph, his son Ralph Jr., and now Jimmy Rubino, all have insisted that they cook in "the Ralph's style."

"We would prefer to train someone to be a chef, teach them right here—than we would to hire some chef with a big ego who thinks he's going to change everything to suit his tastes," **Eddie Rubino** often says. One of Ralph's legendary chefs was **John Teti**, who came to the restaurant in 1941 and stayed until the mid-60's. In 1956, the restaurant sponsored two young chefs from Italy—Rico and Daniel (their last names lost to history). In return for the sponsorship, each man had to stay for at least three years. Rico stayed for seven years, Daniel got homesick and returned to his homeland.

*     *     *

Ralph Sr. was affectionately known as "Poppy" and is lovingly referred to by that name to this day. He passed away on January 10, 1971, at the age of 81. He was three years old when his parents arrived in the United States.

\*     \*     \*

The third floor of the building served as a hotel for many years—and the whole building was a boarding house when **Francesco Dispigno** bought it in 1915. (An old sign advertised Ralph's as a "restaurant and hotel," though we doubt the Bellevue was ever worried.) Many waiters and cooks—and immigrants seeking work—found a "home" in the small rooms here. The rooms were finally removed three years ago and a third-floor dining room was added, allowing us to serve private parties of as many as 40 people.

\*     \*     \*

There was once a side entrance to the restaurant, and a hallway that led to the second and third floor rooms. **Ralph Dispigno, Jr.** remembers spending time playing in those narrow hallways as a child. The Dispigno family lived at 754 S. 9th Street for many years.

\*     \*     \*

When *Palumbo's* and their private CR Club was flourishing just down the street, Ralph's became a gathering place for show business celebrities and *Palumbo's* employees. It was not unusual for the restaurant to be serving dinners to a full dining room of people at 4:30 a.m. in those days.

\*     \*     \*

The Republican National Convention was held in Philadelphia in 1900, the same year that Francesco opened his restaurant. **Theodore Roosevelt** placed the name of **William McKinley** in nomination for the presidency and found his way to Ralph's for some refreshment following the hectic politicking going on in town. The Republicans came back exactly 100 years later for another Convention. Theodore Roosevelt did not attend.

*   *   *

Ralph's patrons are known for their "cool" while dining in the presence of the celebrities who frequent the restaurant. But, once they lost it. Philadelphia Flyers superstar **Eric Lindros**, a frequent diner at the restaurant, came with his family to meet fellow Flyer **Paul Coffey** for dinner. For some reason, diners decided that they needed to get Lindros's signature and they began to follow him. Finally, and before Coffey even got there, Lindros had to leave. "That never happens," lamented Jimmy Rubino Jr., "but Lindros just seemed to get them excited."

*   *   *

"A website and an e-mail address. Yeah, we didn't believe it either," Rubino has been heard to say. The Ralph's Restaurant website (www.ralphsrestaurant.com) carries the complete Ralph's story, pictures, news items, frequently added recipes, our menu, and an informative wine list (not only what we have, but where the wine originated and the best food to serve it with.) A guest book allows people from all over the world to tell us what they think about the restaurant. A full chapter of this book reflects the thoughts and recollections of our many friends.

*   *   *

In March 2000, Chef Rubino and four other members of the Ralph's staff took their food and talents to Chester County, Pa., to serve the annual Charities Dinner for the Tel Hai Retirement Community. "It was a chance to give back to the community and we feel that is an important part of our mission," Rubino said. **Ms. Terri McGovern Potrako,** director of community relations at Tel Hai, said, "It was a wonderful thing that they did for us, and our residents and benefactors were especially grateful." While at Tel Hai, Rubino had a chance to meet with five residents who were

100 years old, or older. "We met one woman who was 105," Rubino said, "can you believe that she was a little girl when my Great-Grandfather started Ralph's? I was thrilled to meet her."

A few weeks before the dinner, Daily News columnist **Stu Bykofsky** shook up Philadelphia with the following headlined item:— **"Ralph's Leaving South Philly"**. . . "Now that I have your attention," Stu wrote, "the 100-year-old Ralph's is leaving South Philly—but only for a day and for a good cause. Chef/owner Jimmy Rubino and four servers will donate their skills to prepare a complete dinner package for the annual "charities dinner" at Tel Hai . . . " Two things happened. People called Ralph's to find out if it was true that the restaurant was leaving town (clearly having only read the headline) and the folks at Tel Hai assumed they were going to have to drive to South Philadelphia to attend the annual event.

P.S. The dinner was a huge success, and South Philly native and noted Author and Surgeon **Dr. Leo Frangipane**, who was the guest speaker that night, said ". . . I can now die a happy man, having eaten Ralph's food again."

*     *     *

## Quotable . . .

". . . Like the Liberty Bell, Billy Penn, Independence Hall, and the late Frank Rizzo, Ralph's is a Philadelphia Institution . . . It was born with the (20th) Century when Italian-born Francesco Dispigno opened his restaurant and named it for his ten-year-old son . . . It has withstood two world wars, the Great Depression, recessions, the Philadelphia restaurant renaissance of the 70's, and the restaurant explosion of the 90's—and it is still here and owned by the same family . . . It's the kind of place where you can close your eyes and take one bite of the eggplant parmesan or linguine with crabmeat and you're transported back to your Nonna's kitchen . . ."
—Phyllis Stein-Novack, South Philadelphia Review, October 4, 1999

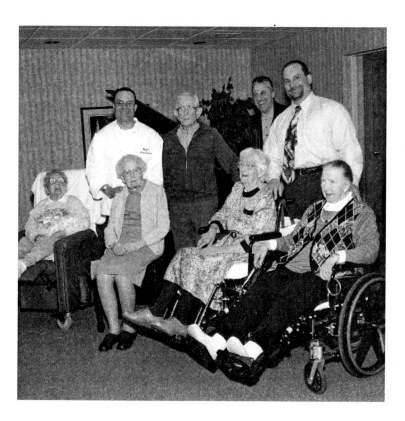

Around as long as Ralph's—
Five 100-year-old or older residents from the Tel Hai Retirement
Community pictured March 22, 2000 with Jimmy Rubino,
Ron Trombino and Eddie Rubino.

Connie Mack, 2nd from right, helps Judge Eugene Bonniwell, 2nd from left, enjoy his birthday cake. Ralph Dispigno, right, smiles approvingly.

A Dispigno Family Event

Ralph hosts veterans from the Valley Forge
Military Hospital in 1951.

# CHAPTER 6

## *Appetizers . . .*

*The American College Dictionary defines "Appetizer" as the food or drink that stimulates the desire to eat. Let's begin this chapter with an Antipasto (ahn-tee-PAHS-toh): Literally meaning, 'before the meal'—hors d'oeuvre, or a first course.*

## ANTIPASTO DI FROMAGE

". . . This appetizer goes great with a nice bottle of wine, like a Cabernet or a Barolo . . ."

1 HEAD ROMAINE

½ LB. FRESH MOZZARELLA

½ LB. PROVOLONE

½ LB. BEL PIASE

½ LB. GORGONZOLA

½ LB. ASIAGO

1 CUP SUN DRIED TOMATOES

½ CUP GREEN OLIVES

½ CUP BLACK OLIVES

½ CUP BALSAMIC VINEGAR

½ CUP EXTRA VIRGIN OLIVE OIL

SALT (TO TASTE)

BLACK PEPPER (TO TASTE)

GARLIC POWDER (TO TASTE)

**Note:** If these cheeses are not available, use any 5 italian cheeses that are available.

SLICE, WASH, AND DRAIN ROMAINE THOROUGHLY. SLICE CHEESES INTO 1-INCH BY ½-INCH SQUARES. ARRANGE ROMAINE ON LARGE, FLAT, SERVING PLATE, AND PLACE CHEESES, SUN DRIED TOMATOES, AND OLIVES ON ROMAINE IN A DECORATIVE FASHION. DRESS WITH OLIVE OIL, BALSAMIC VINEGAR, AND SEASONINGS.

SERVES 4 TO 6.

## *WHAT THEY MEAN . . .*

**Al Dente** - (ahl DEN-teh) literally "to the tooth." Term used to describe the point at which pasta is properly cooked; it has the quality of being slightly underdone or resistant. This term is not to be confused with—nor is Al the brother of—Sam Dente, an infielder with five different American League baseball teams between 1947 and 1955.

# ANTIPASTO

". . . There are many variations to this dish. This version is the traditional recipe that Ralph's has been serving for one hundred years . . ."

1 HEAD ICEBERG LETTUCE

2 LARGE TOMATOES (SLICED INTO ¼ INCH SLICES)

1 MEDIUM CUCUMBER (SLICED INTO ¼ INCH SLICES)

1 SMALL CAN OF BEETS (DRAINED)

6 RADISHES (SLICED THIN)

1 MEDIUM CARROT (SLICED THIN)

1 LARGE RED ONION (SLICED THIN)

6 SLICES IMPORTED PROSCIUTTO

6 SLICES IMPORTED SALAMI

6 ¼-INCH THICK CHUNKS IMPORTED PROVOLONE

12 ANCHOVIES

1 CAN CHUNK TUNA FISH

2 HARD-BOILED EGGS (QUARTERED)

1 SMALL CAN PIMENTOS (DRAINED)

½ CUP RED WINE VINEGAR

½ CUP EXTRA VIRGIN OLIVE OIL

SALT (TO TASTE)

BLACK PEPPER (TO TASTE)

GARLIC POWDER (TO TASTE)

SLICE, WASH, AND DRAIN LETTUCE. MOUND LET-
TUCE ON LARGE, FLAT, SERVING PLATE. LAYER REMAIN-
ING INGREDIENTS ON TOP OF LETTUCE IN A DECO-
RATIVE FASHION. DRESS WITH OLIVE OIL, VINEGAR
AND SEASONINGS.

SERVES 4 TO 6.

## *WHAT THEY MEAN...*

**Baccala** - (bahk-kah-lah): dried salted cod. Also, a key phrase in
the popular Louis Prima tune, Zooma Zooma Baccala (Angelina).

# BRUCHETTA (MODERN)

3 MEDIUM PLUM TOMATOES (CUT INTO CUBES)

½ MEDIUM RED ONION (SLICED)

¼ CUP EXTRA VIRGIN OLIVE OIL

1 TEASPOON RAW GARLIC (MINCED)

12 FRESH BASIL LEAVES (CHOPPED)

½ TEASPOON SALT

½ TEASPOON BLACK PEPPER

½ TEASPOON OREGANO

1 LOAF ITALIAN BREAD (CRUSTY)

MIX ALL INGREDIENTS IN BOWL, EXCEPT BREAD. SLICE ITALIAN BREAD INTO 12 1-INCH SLICES AND SET ON FLAT SHEET PAN. TOAST IN BROILER ON BOTH SIDES UNTIL BREAD IS GOLDEN BROWN AND CRISPY. TOP WITH MIXTURE (ABOUT 1 TABLESPOON EACH) AND SERVE AS SOON AS POSSIBLE.

SERVES 4 TO 6.

# BRUCHETTA (ROASTED PEPPER)

4 ROASTED PEPPERS (SEE RECIPE PG. 77, CUT INTO CUBES)

¼ CUP EXTRA VIRGIN OLIVE OIL

1 TABLESPOON COOKED GARLIC (SEE RECIPE PG. 93)

12 FRESH BASIL LEAVES (CHOPPED)

½ TEASPOON SALT

½ TEASPOON BLACK PEPPER

½ TEASPOON OREGANO

6 TEASPOONS PECORINO ROMANO CHEESE (GRATED)

1 LOAF ITALIAN BREAD (CRUSTY)

IN MIXING BOWL, ADD ALL INGREDIENTS EXCEPT BREAD AND CHEESE. SLICE ITALIAN BREAD INTO 1 INCH SLICES AND PLACE ON FLAT SHEET PAN. TOP BREAD WITH MIXTURE (ABOUT 1 TABLESPOON EACH) AND CHEESE. BAKE IN PREHEATED OVEN AT 350 DEGREES FOR 20 MINUTES.

SERVES 4 TO 6

# BRUCHETTA (TRADITIONAL)

16 OZ. CAN PLUM TOMATOES (DRAINED AND CRUSHED
  BY HAND)
¼ CUP EXTRA VIRGIN OLIVE OIL
12 BASIL LEAVES (CHOPPED)
2 TABLESPOONS COOKED GARLIC (SEE RECIPE PG. 93)
½ TEASPOON SALT
½ TEASPOON BLACK PEPPER
½ TEASPOON OREGANO
6 TEASPOONS PECORINO ROMANO CHEESE (GRATED)
1 LOAF ITALIAN BREAD (CRUSTY)

IN MIXING BOWL, ADD ALL INGREDIENTS EXCEPT
BREAD AND CHEESE. MIX WELL. SLICE ITALIAN BREAD
INTO 12 1-INCH SLICES AND LAY OUT ON FLAT SHEET
PAN. TOP BREAD WITH MIXTURE (ABOUT A TABLE-
SPOON ON EACH) AND CHEESE. PLACE PAN IN PRE-
HEATED OVEN AT 350 DEGREES AND BAKE FOR 20
MINUTES.
  SERVES 4 TO 6.

# CALAMARI

". . . Nowadays, you see a lot of restaurants deep frying Calamari and it's delicious that way, but this is our one-hundred-year-old recipe of cooking it in marinara sauce or, as Italians like to say, 'Gravy' . . ."

## CALAMARI IN RED SAUCE

5 LB. CLEANED CALAMARI (BODIES AND TENTACLES)

3 QTS. MARINARA SAUCE (SEE MARINARA RECIPE PG. 176)


CUT CALAMARI BODIES INTO 1-INCH THICK RINGS. ADD MARINARA SAUCE AND CALAMARI TO 6 QT. POT. BRING TO A BOIL, LOWER FLAME, AND SIMMER FOR 1 HOUR OR UNTIL CALAMARI IS TENDER. (COOKING TIMES VARY).

SERVES 4 TO 6.

## *WHAT THEY MEAN . . .*

**Medigan** (medi-GONN) - Somebody who isn't Italian. Started out to be "American," but something got lost in the translation. Can also be used as part of the sentence . . . ". . . he isn't Italian, that's a too bad . . . he's a Medigan . . . " (Rigoletta Cianci upon learning that Granddaughter Cindy DeMarco's boyfriend was not Italian).

# ESCARGOTS AU GRATIN

24 MEDIUM SIZE SNAILS

4 OUNCES BUTTER

4 SMALL GARLIC CLOVES (MINCED)

2 OUNCES BRANDY

WORCESTERSHIRE SAUCE

TABASCO SAUCE

1 TEASPOON BLACK PEPPER

2 TABLESPOONS PECORINO ROMANO CHEESE (GRATED)

2 TEASPOONS DRY TARRAGON LEAVES

PLACE 6 SNAILS EACH IN FOUR 3-INCH CROCKS. ADD 1 OZ. BUTTER TO EACH CROCK. ADD REMAINING INGREDIENTS TO A MIXING BOWL. MIX WELL AND SPOON MIXTURE ON TOP OF SNAILS EVENLY. PLACE CROCKS IN BROILER FOR 3 TO 4 MINUTES OR UNTIL BROWN.

SERVES 4 TO 6.

## *THINGS OF INTEREST*

Did you know that Italian families traditionally eat snails on St. John's Eve (June 24)? They simmer them slowly with garlic, anchovy, tomato, fresh mint, and pepper.

# ESCAROLE WITH GARLIC AND OIL

". . . Escarole has a slightly bitter flavor. Make sure that you wash it several times because it can be very sandy . . ."

2 LARGE HEADS ESCAROLE

2 QTS. WATER

4 LARGE GARLIC CLOVES (MINCED)

¾ CUP OLIVE OIL

1 TABLESPOON SALT

1 TEASPOON BLACK PEPPER

SLICE AND WASH ESCAROLE THOROUGHLY. ADD ES-CAROLE AND WATER TO 4 QT. POT. STEAM FOR 45 MIN-UTES OR UNTIL TENDER (COOKING TIME VARIES). WHILE ESCAROLE IS COOKING, SAUTÉ GARLIC WITH OLIVE OIL IN A FRYING PAN UNTIL GARLIC IS A GOLDEN COLOR. WHEN ESCAROLE IS COOKED, DRAIN WELL IN COLANDER. ADD GARLIC AND OIL, SALT AND BLACK PEPPER. TOSS WELL. SERVE HOT.

SERVES 4 TO 6.

# CALAMARI

". . . For best results, make sure to use young Calamari no bigger than three inches long. They will be more tender this way . . ."

## GRILLED CALAMARI
## AND FRESH WATERCRESS SALAD

16 LARGE BODIED CALAMARI (CLEANED)

1 CUP EXTRA VIRGIN OLIVE OIL

½ TEASPOON SALT

½ TEASPOON BLACK PEPPER

2 LEMONS

½ TEASPOON GARLIC POWDER

MARINATE CALAMARI IN LARGE MIXING BOWL WITH ALL INGREDIENTS FOR 20 MINUTES. PLACE CALAMARI ON HOT GRILL AND COOK ON EACH SIDE FOR 3 MINUTES UNTIL ALL CALAMARI IS COOKED. SET ASIDE.

(RECIPE CONTINUED ON NEXT PAGE.)

# WATERCRESS SALAD

2 BUNCHES FRESH WATERCRESS
1 LARGE TOMATO (CUT INTO WEDGES)
1 LARGE RED ONION (SLICED)
½ CUP EXTRA VIRGIN OLIVE OIL
½ CUP BALSAMIC VINEGAR
½ TEASPOON SALT
½ TEASPOON BLACK PEPPER
½ TEASPOON OREGANO

WASH WATERCRESS THOROUGHLY, SET IN COLANDER TO DRAIN. IN LARGE MIXING BOWL, TOSS WATERCRESS, SLICED TOMATO, RED ONION, AND REMAINING INGREDIENTS. ARRANGE EVENLY ON 4 FLAT SERVING PLATES—WATERCRESS AND ONION ON ONE SIDE, AND FAN OUT 4 **CALAMARI** ON THE OTHER SIDE.

SERVES 4.

# MUSSELS IN RED SAUCE

4 GARLIC CLOVES (MINCED)

½ CUP OLIVE OIL

80 WHITE WATER MUSSELS (WASHED THOROUGHLY)

6 CUPS MARINARA SAUCE (SEE RECIPE PG. 176)

12 OZ. CAN CLAM JUICE

1 TEASPOON BLACK PEPPER

1 TEASPOON RED PEPPER (CRUSHED)

½ CUP FRESH PARSLEY (CHOPPED)

SAUTÉ GARLIC IN OLIVE OIL IN 6 QT. POT UNTIL GOLDEN IN COLOR. ADD MUSSELS, MARINARA SAUCE, AND REMAINING INGREDIENTS. BRING TO A BOIL, LOWER FLAME, AND COOK UNTIL ALL MUSSELS ARE OPEN, STIRRING CONSTANTLY.

SERVES 4 TO 6.

# MUSSELS IN WHITE SAUCE

8 GARLIC CLOVES (MINCED)

½ CUP OLIVE OIL

80 WHITE WATER MUSSELS (WASHED THOROUGHLY)

48 OZ. CANNED CLAM JUICE

1 TEASPOON BLACK PEPPER

1 TEASPOON RED PEPPER (CRUSHED)

½ CUP FRESH PARSLEY (CHOPPED)

SAUTÉ GARLIC IN OLIVE OIL IN 6 QT. POT UNTIL GOLDEN IN COLOR. ADD MUSSELS, CLAM JUICE, AND REMAINING INGREDIENTS. BRING TO A BOIL. LOWER FLAME AND SIMMER UNTIL ALL MUSSELS ARE OPEN, STIRRING CONSTANTLY.

SERVES 4 TO 6.

# ROASTED PEPPERS

". . . What a great smell, when I walk into the restaurant and I smell the peppers roasting. Your whole house will be filled with the fragrance of roasted peppers. You could also serve this with sliced Provolone or Gorgonzola cheese . . ."

8 LARGE RED BELL PEPPERS

2 LARGE GARLIC CLOVES (MINCED)

8 FRESH BASIL LEAVES (CHOPPED)

¼ CUP PARSLEY (CHOPPED)

¼ CUP EXTRA VIRGIN OLIVE OIL

SALT (DASH)

BLACK PEPPER (DASH)

OREGANO (DASH)

SPRAY A FLAT SHEET PAN WITH A NON-STICK SPRAY. ROAST PEPPERS ON A PAN IN PREHEATED OVEN AT 400 DEGREES FOR 1 HOUR, ROTATING WHEN TOPS HAVE A CHARRED LOOK TO THEM. WHEN PEPPERS ARE FINISHED, PLACE IN A BROWN BAG FOR 30 MINUTES (THIS WILL CAUSE THE SKIN TO BE PEELED EASIER). PEEL SKIN OFF PEPPERS AND TEAR INTO STRIPS. PLACE PEPPERS AND REMAINING INGREDIENTS IN BOWL AND TOSS UNTIL PEPPERS ARE COATED.

SERVES 4 TO 6.

# SEAFOOD ANTIPASTO

1 HEAD ROMAINE

2 HEADS RADDICHIO

12 JUMBO SHRIMP

16 WHITE WATER MUSSELS

½ LB. JUMBO LUMP CRABMEAT

12 OZ. SALMON FILET

2-6 OZ. CANS CHUNK TUNA FISH

1 LARGE RED ONION (SLICED THIN)

16 SMALL CHERRY TOMATOES

PEEL AND CLEAN SHRIMP (SAVE THE SHELLS FOR DRESSING). BOIL SHRIMP FOR 4 MINUTES IN SAUCE POT. POUR SHRIMP INTO COLANDER AND RINSE UNDER COLD WATER UNTIL COOL.

WASH MUSSELS THOROUGHLY AND STEAM IN SAUCE POT WITH ABOUT 1 INCH OF WATER AT BOTTOM OF POT, UNTIL ALL MUSSELS ARE OPENED. POUR MUSSELS INTO COLANDER AND RINSE UNDER COLD WATER UNTIL COOL.

CUT SALMON INTO 4 EQUAL PIECES, PLACE ON FLAT SHEET PAN, AND BAKE IN PREHEATED OVEN FOR 20 MINUTES AT 350 DEGREES. LET FISH COOL TO ROOM TEMPERATURE.

OPEN AND DRAIN TUNA FISH.

SLICE ROMAINE THIN AND WASH THOROUGHLY,

DRAIN WELL. SLICE RADDICHIO THIN AND WASH THOROUGHLY, DRAIN WELL.

MIX ROMAINE AND RADDICHIO AND PLACE EQUAL AMOUNTS ON 4 SERVING PLATES. TOP WITH SLICED ONION AND 4 TOMATOES. ARRANGE 3 SHRIMP, 4 MUSSELS, 1 PIECE SALMON, AND DIVIDE CRABMEAT AND TUNA INTO 4 EQUAL SERVINGS FOR EACH PLATE.

SERVES 4.

## *WHAT THEY MEAN . . .*

**Cacciatora** - (kah-chah-TOH-ra) means "hunters style." It is meat or fish cooked in a sauce that includes tomatoes, mushrooms, Rosemary, and red or white wine.

# SEAFOOD ANTIPASTO DRESSING

SHELLS FROM SHRIMP
1 ½ PINTS HEAVY CREAM
2 TABLESPOONS COOKED GARLIC (SEE RECIPE PG. 93)
1 TEASPOON SALT
½ TEASPOON BLACK PEPPER
½ TEASPOON OREGANO

IN MEDIUM SAUCEPOT, BRING ALL INGREDIENTS TO A BOIL. LOWER FLAME AND SIMMER FOR 1 HOUR, STIRRING CONSTANTLY. STRAIN LIQUID THROUGH A STRAINER AND LET COOL OVER NIGHT IN REFRIGERATOR. SERVE ON ANTIPASTO.

## *THINGS OF INTEREST*

Former Philadelphia Mayor and Police Commissioner, the legendary Frank Rizzo, was born in South Philadelphia in 1920. He was a frequent guest at Ralph's during his long and colorful career. South Philly's population at the time of his birth was 375,000.

# CHAPTER 7

## *Salads*

*At the dawn of the Renaissance in the 14ᵗʰ Century, a meal was very light except in wealthy families. In the middle class, the meal would begin with either fruit (generally melon) or salad, followed by the main meat or poultry, and conclude with goat cheese, grapes, or figs. It wasn't until late in the 15ᵗʰ Century that pasta became an Italian staple. The tradition of fruit or a salad before the main meal is followed to this day.*

## FRESH ARUGULA SALAD

". . . If you are not familiar with the flavor of Arugula it has a peppery taste and the sweetness of Balsamic Vinegar compliments it very well . . ."

1 BUNCH FRESH ARUGULA (WASHED THOROUGHLY)

1 HEAD RADICCHIO

1 BELGIAN ENDIVE

½ CUP EXTRA VIRGIN OLIVE OIL

½ CUP BALSAMIC VINEGAR

SALT (PINCH)

BLACK PEPPER (PINCH)

GARLIC POWDER (PINCH)

1 RED ONION (SLICED THIN)

IN MIXING BOWL, TOSS ARUGULA, RED ONION, OLIVE OIL, BALSAMIC VINEGAR, AND SEASONINGS. ARRANGE RADICCHIO AND ENDIVE AROUND OUTSIDE OF A FLAT SERVING PLATE AND PLACE ARUGULA AND ONION IN THE MIDDLE.

      SERVES 2.

## *WHAT THEY MEAN . . .*

**Booro** - (BOOR-ro) means butter (it is not a small horse-like animal).
**Brodo** - (BROH-do) means broth.
**Brodetto** - (broh-DET-toh) is a soup generally containing pieces of fish.
**Battuto** - (baht-TOO-toh) is a base for soups, stews, etc. It is made of finely chopped vegetables, herbs, and salt pork or oil.

# CAESAR SALAD

8 ANCHOVIES

4 GARLIC CLOVES (MINCED)

1 TABLESPOON PECORINO ROMANO CHEESE (GRATED)

3 EGG YOLKS

1 TABLESPOON WORCESTERSHIRE SAUCE

1 TEASPOON TABASCO

1 TABLESPOON DIJON MUSTARD

1 LEMON (CUT IN HALF SEEDS REMOVED)

BLACK PEPPER (PINCH)

OREGANO (PINCH)

2 ½ CUPS VEGETABLE OIL

2 HEADS ROMAINE

MASH ANCHOVIES IN MIXING BOWL. ADD REMAINING INGREDIENTS AND MIX WELL. AT THIS POINT, ADD OIL VERY SLOWLY AND WHISK A LITTLE AT A TIME UNTIL ALL OIL IS USED AND DRESSING IS THICK. (NOTE: YOU MUST ADD OIL VERY SLOWLY OR THE DRESSING WILL BREAK.) SLICE, WASH, AND DRAIN ROMAINE. ADD DRESSING.

SERVES 4 TO 6 SALADS.

# FRESH STRING BEAN SALAD

"... This dish is a great summertime appetizer or can be served as a side dish with a sandwich or other entrée ..."

2 LBS. FRESH STRING BEANS

2 QTS. WATER

1 LARGE RED ONION (SLICED THIN)

¾ CUP RED WINE VINEGAR

¾ CUP VEGETABLE OIL

4 GARLIC CLOVES (MINCED)

¾ TEASPOON SALT

½ TEASPOON BLACK PEPPER

½ TEASPOON OREGANO


WASH AND STEM STRING BEANS. COOK IN 2 QTS. BOILING WATER UNTIL TENDER (ABOUT 3 TO 5 MINUTES. DO NOT OVER COOK). POUR INTO COLANDER AND RUN UNDER COLD WATER UNTIL COOL. REFRIGERATE FOR 2 HOURS. PUT STRING BEANS INTO LARGE SERVING BOWL AND ADD ONIONS, VINEGAR, OIL, GARLIC, AND SEASONINGS, AND TOSS VERY WELL.

SERVES 4 TO 6.

# HEARTS OF ARTICHOKE SALAD

1 LARGE HEAD LETTUCE
20 IMPORTED ARTICHOKE HEARTS (QUARTERED)
1 LARGE RED ONION (SLICED THIN)
1 CUP OLIVE OIL
1 CUP VINEGAR
SALT (DASH)
BLACK PEPPER (DASH)
GARLIC POWDER (DASH)
OREGANO (DASH)

SLICE, WASH, AND DRAIN LETTUCE. MOUND LETTUCE ON FLAT SERVING PLATE. ARRANGE ARTICHOKE HEARTS ON TOP OF LETTUCE. PUT ONIONS ON TOP. DRESS WITH OLIVE OIL, VINEGAR, SALT, BLACK PEPPER, AND GARLIC POWDER.
SERVES 4 TO 6.

## *WHAT THEY MEAN . . .*

**Cannoli** - (kah-NO-lee). Tubes of crisp pastry filled with ricotta cheese, chocolate, and candied fruit.
**Tartufi** - (tar-TOO-fee). Truffles.

## RALPH'S TOSSED SALAD

". . . This salad has great 'eye appeal' because of all the different colors. It is a great way to start a meal . . ."

1 HEAD ICEBERG LETTUCE
2 LARGE TOMATOES (SLICED INTO ¼ INCH SLICES)
1 MEDIUM CUCUMBER (SLICED INTO ¼ INCH SLICES)
1 SMALL CAN BEETS (DRAINED)
6 RADISHES (SLICED THIN)
1 LARGE CARROT (SLICED THIN)
1 LARGE RED ONION (SLICED THIN)

SLICE, WASH, AND DRAIN LETTUCE. MOUND LETTUCE IN LARGE SERVING BOWL. ARRANGE REMAINING INGREDIENTS ON TOP OF LETTUCE IN A DECORATIVE FASHION. DRESS WITH BALSAMIC VINEGAR DRESSING (SEE RECIPE PG. 87).

SERVES 4 TO 6.

## *WHAT THEY MEAN . . .*

**Contorni** - (kohn-TOR-nee). Vegetables accompanying the main course, or it could mean garnishes.

# CHAPTER 8

## Dressings, Stocks, and Soups

*In this chapter, we'll look at some old-time Italian "staples." How to make a great dressing, how to prepare stocks and recipes for my Grandmother's "cure-all" Chicken Soup, and my personal favorite, Italian Wedding Soup.*

## BALSAMIC VINEGAR AND OLIVE OIL DRESSING

16 OZ. BALSAMIC VINEGAR

16 OZ. EXTRA VIRGIN OLIVE OIL

1 TABLESPOON BLACK PEPPER

1 TABLESPOON SALT

1 TABLESPOON OREGANO

1 TABLESPOON GARLIC POWDER

1 TABLESPOON DRY BASIL

MIX INGREDIENTS IN MIXING BOWL. FUNNEL INTO 32 OZ. BOTTLE. THIS BOTTLE SHOULD BE ENOUGH TO DRESS 15 TO 20 SALADS. KEEP REFRIGERATED AND SHAKE WELL BEFORE EACH USE.

Ralph Dispigno, himself

# RALPH'S EGG DRESSING

**". . . This was my Grandfather Ralph's favorite salad dressing and, of course, his own personal recipe for it . . ."**

3 HARD BOILED EGGS (BOIL EGGS FOR 5 MINUTES. RINSE IN COLD WATER UNTIL EGGS ARE COOL. PEEL SHEELS OFF.)

2 CUPS KETCHUP

4 CUPS VEGETABLE OIL

3 TABLESPOONS WORCESTERSHIRE SAUCE

2 TABLESPOONS TABASCO

1 TABLESPOON PECORINO ROMANO CHEESE (GRATED)

1 TEASPOON BLACK PEPPER

1 TEASPOON OREGANO

2 LEMON HALVES (REMOVE SEEDS)

CRUSH EGGS WITH A FORK IN MIXING BOWL. ADD REMAINING INGREDIENTS AND WHISK UNTIL THICK. WILL BE ENOUGH TO DRESS 8 TO 10 SALADS.

# GORGONZOLA CHEESE DRESSING

1 PINT HEAVY CREAM

¼ LB. GORGONZOLA CHEESE

1 TABLESPOON COOKED GARLIC (SEE RECIPE PG. 93)

1 TEASPOON SALT

½ TEASPOON BLACK PEPPER

½ TEASPOON OREGANO

6 FRESH BASIL LEAVES (CHOPPED)

CRUMBLE CHEESE INTO LITTLE PIECES. IN SMALL SAUCE POT, BRING ALL INGREDIENTS TO A BOIL. LOWER FLAME AND SIMMER FOR 10 MINUTES. LET COOL AND REFRIGERATE OVER NIGHT. WILL MAKE ENOUGH TO DRESS 6 TO 8 SALADS.

## *THINGS OF INTEREST*

Gorgonzola cheese, lightly spiced and sharp, ranks with the greatest veined cheeses. It is a stracchino, meaning it is made from the milk of "tired" cows that had been grazing on the slopes of the Alps. At one time, many such cows wintered in Gorgonzola (near Milan) and there this masterpiece evolved. Today it is produced mostly in the Po River flatlands.

# OIL AND VINEGAR DRESSING

*". . . When a basic oil and vinegar dressing is needed . . ."*

16 OZ. RED WINE VINEGAR

16 OZ VEGETABLE OIL

1 TABLESPOON BLACK PEPPER

1 TABLESPOON SALT

1 TABLESPOON OREGANO

1 TABLESPOON GARLIC POWDER


MIX INGREDIENTS IN MIXING BOWL. FUNNEL INTO 32 OZ. BOTTLE. THIS BOTTLE SHOULD BE ENOUGH TO DRESS 15 TO 20 SALADS. KEEP REFRIGERATED. SHAKE WELL BEFORE EACH USE.

# ROASTED PEPPER DRESSING

6 LARGE ROASTED PEPPERS (SEE RECIPE PG. 77)

4 OZ. PHILADELPHIA CREAM CHEESE

½ CUP WATER

1 PINT HEAVY CREAM

1 TEASPOON SALT

½ TEASPOON BLACK PEPPER

½ TEASPOON OREGANO

PUREE ROASTED PEPPERS AND CREAM CHEESE WITH WATER. POUR INTO MEDIUM MIXING BOWL. WHISK IN CREAM (WHISK LIGHTLY OR CREAM WILL START TO THICKEN). ADD REMAINING INGREDIENTS. WILL MAKE ENOUGH TO DRESS 6 TO 8 SALADS.

# COOKING GARLIC

". . . brings out its sweetness and tones down the bitterness. As you will see, we use cooked garlic in 98% of the recipes at Ralph's. Make it up ahead of time and keep it refrigerated, ready to use whenever a recipe calls for it . . ."

COOKED GARLIC

40 PEELED GARLIC CLOVES

5 CUPS VEGETABLE OIL

PEEL FRESH GARLIC UNTIL YOU HAVE ABOUT 40 CLOVES. MINCE IN FOOD PROCESSOR. ADD 4 CUPS OF OIL TO LARGE FRY PAN. HEAT OIL ON MEDIUM FLAME. TEST OIL BY ADDING A SMALL AMOUNT OF GARLIC. ONCE OIL IS HOT, ADD MINCED GARLIC, AND LOWER FLAME. SAUTÉ GARLIC UNTIL GOLDEN IN COLOR. POUR INTO METAL CONTAINER AND ADD LAST CUP OF OIL TO STOP COOKING PROCESS. COOL, THEN REFRIGERATE. WILL LAST FOR WEEKS IN FRIDGE. USE WHENEVER NEEDED·IN OUR RECIPES.

# RUE

". . . you will see most of the butter dishes call for rue. What rue does is thicken the dish, so it is very important to use it when a recipe calls for it . . ."

## RUE RECIPE

16 0Z. CHICKEN BROTH

6 ROUNDED TABLESPOONS FLOUR

4 OZ. WATER

1 TEASPOON KITCHEN BOUQUET (FOR COLOR)


IN MIXING BOWL, ADD FLOUR AND KITCHEN BOU-QUET TO THE WATER WHILE WHISKING (THIS MIX-TURE MUST BE SMOOTH WITH NO LUMPS). BRING CHICKEN BROTH TO A BOIL. WHEN BROTH IS BOIL-ING, WHISK IN FLOUR MIXTURE, AGAIN MAKING SURE THERE ARE NO LUMPS. ALLOW TO COOL, THEN RE-FRIGERATE. WILL LAST FOR ABOUT 2 WEEKS OR CAN BE FROZEN AND DEFROSTED WHEN NEEDED.

# VEAL STOCK (1ST STEP)

5 LB. VEAL BONES

2 LARGE CARROTS (SLICED)

4 CELERY STALKS (SLICED)

2 LARGE SPANISH ONIONS (SLICED)

1 CUP FRESH PARSLEY (CHOPPED)

½ CUP VEGETABLE OIL

1 CUP WATER

IN LARGE BAKING PAN, ROAST ALL INGREDIENTS IN PREHEATED OVEN AT 375 DEGREES FOR 1 HOUR, OR UNTIL BONES ARE BROWNED AND LIQUID AT BOTTOM OF PAN IS EVAPORATED.

# (2ND STEP)

4 QTS. WATER

2 TABLESPOON SALT

1 TABLESPOON BLACK PEPPER

2 TABLESPOONS CORN STARCH

1/2 CUP WATER

PUT ALL INGREDIENTS IN LARGE POT AND SCRAPE BOTTOM OF ROASTING PAN. ADD SCRAPINGS TO POT WITH 4 QTS. WATER, 2 TABLESPOONS SALT, AND 1 TABLESPOON BLACK PEPPER. BRING TO A BOIL AND

SIMMER ON LOW FLAME FOR 1 ½ HOURS. STRAIN LIQ-UID THROUGH A STRAINER INTO ANOTHER POT AND PUT BACK ON STOVE ON LOW FLAME. MIX 2 TABLE-SPOONS OF CORN STARCH WITH ½ CUP WATER IN SMALL MIXING BOWL. WHEN STOCK RETURNS TO A BOIL, WHISK CORN STARCH MIXTURE IN UNTIL LIQ-UID STARTS TO THICKEN (YOU MAY NOT HAVE TO USE ALL THE CORN STARCH MIXTURE). TASTE TO SEE IF STOCK NEEDS MORE SALT, ADD IF NECESSARY.

THIS STOCK CAN BE USED AS A SAUCE FOR VEAL, OR ADD VEGETABLES AND USE AS SOUP.

## THINGS OF INTEREST

In 1900, the year Ralph's opened, South Philadelphia had 282,000 residents. A boat trip to the United States from Sicily cost $30 in 1910, and in 1912 South Philadelphia's first public library opened at Fifth & Ellsworth.

# CHICKEN SOUP

". . . Whenever my Brother Eddie or I had a cold, Nanny (Mary Dispigno) came to the rescue with Chicken Soup. This Soup had a way of making you feel better . . ."

1 WHOLE CHICKEN

3 QUARTS WATER

1 LARGE SPANISH ONION (CHOPPED)

2 LARGE CARROTS (SLICED)

4 CELERY STALKS (SLICED)

2 TABLESPOONS SALT

1 TABLESPOON BLACK PEPPER

1 BUNCH PARSLEY

¾ CUP PERCORINO ROMANO CHEESE (GRATED)

WASH CHICKEN THOROUGHLY, CUT IN HALF AND QUARTER EACH HALF. PUT ALL INGREDIENTS IN 6 QT. SAUCE POT. BRING TO A BOIL, LOWER FLAME, AND SIMMER FOR 1 ½ HOURS. AFTER SOUP IS DONE, STRAIN THROUGH A MESH STRAINER INTO ANOTHER POT AND STRAIN FAT OFF OF TOP WITH LADLE. SHRED CHICKEN AND ADD TO SOUP. ALSO ADD SOME CHOPPED CARROT, ONION, AND CELERY. SERVE WITH PASTINE (SEE RECIPE PG. 108). TOP WITH ROMANO CHEESE.

# ROASTED GARLIC SOUP

3 - 28 OZ. CANS OF WHOLE PEELED TOMATOES
   (CRUSHED BY HAND)

1 LARGE SPANISH ONION (CHOPPED)

2 CUPS OF CREAM

1 TABLESPOON OF BLACK PEPPER

1 TABLESPOON OF SALT

12 FRESH BASIL LEAVES (CHOPPED)

6 GARLIC CLOVES (MINCED)

16 GARLIC CLOVES (WHOLE)

½ CUP EXTRA VIRGIN OLIVE OIL

½ CUP FRESH PARSLEY (CHOPPED)

SAUTÉ ONION AND GARLIC WITH ½ CUP OF EXTRA VIRGIN OIL IN 4 QT. SAUCE POT. WHEN ONION IS TRANSPARENT AND GARLIC IS TURNING A GOLDEN COLOR, ADD CRUSHED TOMATOES, BRING TO A BOIL, THEN COOK ON LOW FLAME FOR 40 MINUTES, STIR-RING CONSTANTLY. WHILE SOUP IS COOKING, ROAST 16 WHOLE GARLIC CLOVES (COATED WITH OLIVE OIL) IN OVEN FOR 30 MINUTES AT 350 DEGREES.

AFTER SOUP HAS COOKED FOR 40 MINUTES, ADD 2 CUPS OF CREAM, 12 BASIL LEAVES, SALT, AND BLACK PEPPER. COOK ANOTHER 15 MINUTES. SERVE IN FOUR LARGE SOUP BOWLS—ADDING 4 ROASTED GARLIC CLOVES TO EACH BOWL. TOP WITH CHOPPED PARS-LEY. SERVE WITH TOASTED ITALIAN BREAD.

SERVES 4 TO 6.

**Note:** This also makes a wonderful sauce for either chicken or veal.

## ESCAROLE AND BEANS SOUP

1 LARGE SPANISH ONION (CHOPPED)

6 TO 8 GARLIC CLOVES (MINCED)

1 CUP EXTRA VIRGIN OLIVE OIL

1 LB. BAG GREAT NORTHERN BEANS (RINSED)

1 HEAD ESCAROLE (SLICED AND WASHED)    ·

3 QT. WATER

2 LARGE CARROTS (DICED)

3 CELERY STALKS (DICED)

4 CUPS MARINARA SAUCE (SEE MARINARA RECIPE PG. 176)

SMALL BUNCH FRESH BASIL (CHOPPED)

IF FRESH NOT AVAILABLE, USE 1 TEASPOON DRY BASIL

1 ½ TABLESPOON SALT

1 TEASPOON BLACK PEPPER

¾ CUP PECORINO ROMANO CHEESE (GRATED)

SAUTÉ ONION AND GARLIC IN OLIVE OIL IN 4 QT. POT UNTIL GOLDEN IN COLOR. ADD REMAINING INGREDIENTS. BRING TO A BOIL, LOWER FLAME, AND SIMMER UNTIL BEANS ARE TENDER. SERVE AND TOP WITH ROMANO CHEESE.

SERVES 4 TO 6.

# LENTIL SOUP

1 LARGE SPANISH ONION (CHOPPED)

6 TO 8 LARGE GARLIC CLOVES (MINCED)

1 CUP EXTRA VIRGIN OLIVE OIL

1 LB. BAG OF LENTILS (RINSED)

3 QTS. OF WATER

4 CUPS MARINARA SAUCE (SEE MARINARA RECIPE PG. 176)

3 CELERY STALKS (CHOPPED)

2 LARGE CARROTS (CHOPPED)

1 SMALL BUNCH OF BASIL (CHOPPED)

IF FRESH NOT AVAILABLE, USE 1 TEASPOON DRY

1 ½ TABLESPOONS SALT

1 TEASPOON BLACK PEPPER

¾ CUP PECORINO ROMANO CHEESE (GRATED)

SAUTÉ ONION AND GARLIC WITH OLIVE OIL IN 4QT. POT UNTIL GOLDEN IN COLOR. ADD LENTILS, WATER, MARINARA, CELERY, CARROTS, BASIL, SALT, AND BLACK PEPPER. BRING TO A BOIL, LOWER FLAME, AND SIMMER UNTIL LENTILS ARE TENDER. SERVE WITH TUBETTI.

# MINESTRONE SOUP

**". . . A hearty soup that is also good for you. Try Toasting Italian Bread and serving it in the soup . . ."**

1 LARGE SPANISH ONION (CHOPPED)

6 TO 8 LARGE GARLIC CLOVES (MINCED)

1 CUP EXTRA VIRGIN OLIVE OIL

3 QTS. OF WATER

4 CELERY STALKS (SLICED ¼ INCH THICK)

3 LARGE CARROTS (CUT IN HALF, THEN SLICED ¼ INCH THICK)

4 CUPS MARINARA SAUCE (SEE RECIPE PG. 176)

1 LB. FRESH STRING BEANS (CUT INTO 1 INCH PIECES)

2 MEDIUM SIZE ZUCCHINI (CUT IN HALF, THEN SLICED ¼ INCH THICK)

2 MEDIUM SIZE YELLOW SQUASH (CUT IN HALF, THEN SLICED ¼ INCH THICK)

1 28 OZ. CAN TOMATOES (CRUSHED BY HAND)

1 LARGE HEAD OF ESCAROLE (WASHED AND SLICED THIN)

1 ½ TABLESPOON SALT

1 TEASPOON BLACK PEPPER

¾ CUP PECORINO ROMANO CHEESE (GRATED)

SAUTÉ ONION AND GARLIC IN OLIVE OIL IN 4QT. POT UNTIL GOLDEN IN COLOR. ADD WATER, CELERY, AND CARROT. BRING TO A BOIL AND COOK FOR 10 MINUTES. ADD REMAINING INGREDIENTS AND SIMMER FOR 30 MINUTES OR UNTIL VEGETABLES ARE TENDER. SERVE AND TOP WITH ROMANO CHEESE.

SERVES 4 TO 6.

## *THINGS OF INTEREST*

The Philadelphia Navy Yard opened in South Philadelphia in 1801 and provided jobs to local residents for almost two centuries. Thomas Jefferson lived in South Philly in 1793 while serving as Secretary of State (the U. S. Capitol was then Philadelphia). His three-story home was between Dickinson and Reed Streets.

# PASTA FAGIOLE SOUP

1 LARGE SPANISH ONION (CHOPPED)

6 TO 8 GARLIC CLOVES (MINCED)

1 CUP EXTRA VIRGIN OLIVE OIL

1 LB. BAG GREAT NORTHERN BEANS

4 CUPS MARINARA SAUCE (SEE MARINARA RECIPE PG. 176)

3 QTS. WATER

3 CELERY STALKS (DICED)

2 LARGE CARROTS (DICED)

1 SMALL BUNCH OF BASIL (CHOPPED)

IF FRESH NOT AVAILABLE, USE 1 TEASPOON DRY

1 ½ TABLE SPOONS SALT

1 TEASPOON BLACK PEPPER

¾ CUP PECORINO ROMANO CHEESE (GRATED)

SAUTÉ ONION AND GARLIC IN OLIVE OIL IN 4QT. POT UNTIL GOLDEN IN COLOR. ADD BEANS, MARINARA, WATER, CELERY, CARROTS, BASIL, SALT, AND BLACK PEPPER. BRING TO A BOIL, LOWER FLAME, AND SIMMER UNTIL BEANS ARE TENDER.TOP WITH ROMANO CHEESE.

**Note:** Medigans (see definition elsewhere in this book) always call this dish "Pasta Fazool." Fagioli (fah-JO-lee) means dried kidney beans.

# STRACCIATELLI SOUP

". . . This soup is also called Italian wedding soup. It happens to be my personal favorite . . ."

(SEE CHICKEN SOUP RECIPE PG. 97)
4 EGGS (BEATEN)
1LB. FRESH SPINACH
¾ CUP PECORINO ROMANO CHEESE (GRATED)

FOLLOW CHICKEN SOUP RECIPE. AFTER STRAINING, ADD SHREDDED CHICKEN, CARROTS, CELERY, AND ONION AS USUAL. THEN BRING SOUP BACK TO A BOIL. WHEN BOILING, ADD BEATEN EGGS AND SPINACH. LOWER FLAME AND SIMMER FOR 4 MINUTES, STIRRING CONSTANTLY. SERVE AND TOP WITH ROMANO CHEESE.

SERVES 4 TO 6.

Note: In Italian the word *stracciatella* literally means "little rags," which, if you think about it, is what the egg looks like when it breaks up in little flakes and floats in the broth.

Jack Klugman samples some of Ralph's pasta.

# CHAPTER 9

## Pasta Dishes

*Italians and Pasta are one of the great combinations of all time. It is amazing that they created so many variations of something that is made so simply. PASTA (PAH-stah): basically a dough of flour and water or semolina, used to make noodles—pasta is the generic name for a wide range of products from spaghetti to cannelloni.*

*There are, in fact, more than 40 different pastas commonly used by Italian chefs.*

*Pasta for soup includes: Conchigliette, Anellini, Nocchette, Ancini de Pepe, Semini di Melo, and Tubetti.*

*Pasta to be boiled includes: Fettucine, Fettucine Verdi, Fusilli, Capellini, Fedelini, Spaghetti, Spaghettini, Ziti, Mezzani, Perciatelli, Perciatelloni, Lasagnette, Linguine, Mafaldine, Mafalde, and Penne.*

*Pasta for baking includes: Lasagne, Curly Lasagne, Lasagne Verdi, Occhi di Lupo, Conchiglie, Penne, Rigatoni, Pennini, Cappelletti, Elbow Macaroni, Tortiglioni, Gramigna Rigata, and Farfelle (bows).*

*Pasta to be stuffed includes: Lumache, Agnolotti, Manicotti, Cannelloni, Ravioli, and Tortellini.*

*Now on to some of Ralph's classic adaptations of these varieties of pasta. . . .*

# WHEN MAKING PASTA . . .

. . . or macaroni, as we like to call it, the key is making sure you cook it al dente (hard but not raw). Cooking times vary, so keep tasting to make sure when it's done.

# COOKING PASTA

THIS RECIPE WILL APPLY TO 1LB. OF ANY DRY PASTA.

EXAMPLE: SPAGHETTI, ZITI, PENNE, LINGUINE, PASTINE, TUBETTI, BOW TIES, RIGATONI, ETC.

BRING 6 QTS. WATER AND 2 TABLESPOONS OF SALT TO A BOIL. ADD PASTA AND COOK AL DENTE (OR TO YOUR LIKING). WHEN PASTA IS DONE, DRAIN IN COLANDER. PUT ON SERVING PLATE AND TOP WITH YOUR FAVORITE SAUCE.

# BAKED LASAGNA

4 QTS. WATER

1 TABLESPOON SALT

1 ½ LB. LASAGNA NOODLES

1 CUP VEGETABLE OIL

1 ½ LB. GROUND BEEF

½ LB. SWEET ITALIAN SAUSAGE

3 LB. RICOTTA CHEESE

28 OZ. MARINARA SAUCE (SEE RECIPE PG. 176)

1 ½ CUPS PECORINO ROMANO CHEESE (GRATED)

½ LB. MOZZARELLA (SHREDDED)

BRING NOODLES, SALT, AND 4 QTS. WATER TO A BOIL IN 6 QT. POT. WHILE NOODLES ARE BOILING, SAUTÉ BEEF WITH ½ CUP OIL UNTIL BROWNED. WHEN MEAT IS DONE, DRAIN IN COLANDER. CUT SAUSAGE INTO, 18- ½ INCH PIECES. WITH THE OTHER ½ CUP OIL, SAUTÉ SAUSAGE ON MEDIUM FLAME UNTIL COOKED. REMOVE SAUSAGE FROM PAN ON TO A PAPER TOWEL TO DRAIN OIL. WHEN NOODLES ARE DONE, LEAVE IN POT AND RUN COLD WATER ON THEM UNTIL COOL. LEAVE NOODLES IN WATER SO THEY DO NOT STICK.

COAT BOTTOM OF BAKING PAN WITH 2 CUPS SAUCE (PAN SHOULD BE ABOUT 12 INCHES WIDE BY 10 INCHES LONG BY 3 INCHES DEEP). LAYER A ROW OF NOODLES

ON BOTTOM, THEN A LAYER OF RICOTTA, USING YOUR FINGERS TO SPREAD THE RICOTTA. NEXT, A LAYER OF GROUND BEEF, A LAYER OF MOZZARELLA,SPREAD OUT 6 PIECES OF SAUSAGE, AND THEN ROMANO CHEESE. THIS PROCESS MUST BE DONE 2 MORE TIMES, SO MAKE SURE YOU CONSERVE ENOUGH TO LAST FOR 3 ROWS TOTAL (A TOTAL OF 4 FOR THE NOODLES AND SAUCE—ONE EXTRA FOR THE TOP LAYER). THE PRO-CESS GOES LIKE THIS: SAUCE, NOODLES, RICOTTA, GROUND BEEF, MOZZARELLA, SAUSAGE, THEN ROMANO CHEESE, WITH THE LAST LAYER BEING NOODLES, THEN SAUCE.

COVER WITH FOIL AND BAKE IN PREHEATED OVEN AT 400 DEGREES FOR 1 HOUR.

SERVES 6 TO 8.

## *THINGS OF INTEREST*

The City of Philadelphia sold League Island Park to the U. S. Government for $1 in 1868, hoping the Feds would relocate the Navy Yard there - which they did. The new yard, opened ten years later, filled 800 acres and five miles of waterfront. The Navy's mothball fleet resides there to this day.

Mary Dispigno
(Nanny)

## THIS IS ONE OF MY FAVORITE DISHES

. . . I grew up on this one. Every Friday I would ask my nanny (grandmother) "What's for dinner?" I always hoped she would say crabs and macaroni! Friday was the night Italian Catholics ate seafood because meat wasn't eaten on Friday . . .

## CRABS AND MACARONI

16 LARGE BLUE POINT CRABS (ALIVE)
12 CUPS MARINARA SAUCE (SEE RECIPE PG. 176)
1 LB. LINGUINE (SEE RECIPE PG. 108)

HAVE THE SEAFOOD MARKET WHERE YOU BUY YOUR CRABS CLEAN THEM FOR YOU. IT IS MUCH EASIER AND FOR A SMALL FEE, THEY WILL DO IT FOR YOU. WASH CRABS THOROUGHLY. IN A VERY LARGE SAUCE POT, BRING CRABS AND MARINARA SAUCE TO A BOIL. LOWER FLAME, AND COOK FOR 15 TO 18 MIN-UTES, DEPENDING ON THE SIZE OF THE CRAB, STIR-RING CONSTANTLY. DIVIDE LINGUINE INTO 4 BOWLS, TOP WITH CRAB GRAVY, AND SERVE 4 CRABS ON 4 SEPA-RATE PLATES. (NOTE: YOU WILL NEED A NUTCRACKER TO OPEN THE CRABS. IT CAN GET MESSY, BUT IT IS A LOT OF FUN!)

# LINGUINE PESCATORE RED

8 LARGE GARLIC CLOVES (MINCED)

½ CUP OLIVE OIL

12 JUMBO SHRIMP (SHELL REMOVED, DEVEINED)

16 WHITE WATER MUSSELS

16 LITTLE NECK CLAMS

¼ LB. JUMBO LUMP CRABMEAT

2 CUPS MARINARA SAUCE (SEE RECIPE PG. 176)

16 OZ. CAN CLAM JUICE

1 TEASPOON BLACK PEPPER

1 TEASPOON OREGANO

¼ CUP FRESH PARSLEY (CHOPPED)

1 LB. LINGUINE (SEE RECIPE PG. 108)


SAUTÉ GARLIC IN OLIVE OIL IN 4QT. POT UNTIL GOLDEN IN COLOR, THEN ADD SEAFOOD AND REMAINING INGREDIENTS. BRING TO A BOIL. LOWER FLAME AND SIMMER FOR 12 MINUTES, STIRRING CONSTANTLY. SERVE ON LINGUINE (1LB.),DIVIDED EVENLY INTO 4 BOWLS. LADEL SEAFOOD AND REMAINING SAUCE ON TOP.EACH BOWL GETS 3 SHRIMP, 4 MUSSELS, 4 CLAMS, AND SOME CRABMEAT.

SERVES 4.

SERVE ON BED OF LINGUINE (SEE RECIPE).

# MEAT BALLS

". . . Meatballs can be eaten with your favorite pasta or for lunchtime as a sandwich with Italian bread and grated Romano cheese . . ."

½ LOAF ITALIAN BREAD

WATER (ENOUGH TO DAMPEN BREAD)

1 ½ LB. GROUND BEEF, VEAL, AND PORK (MIXED)

5 LARGE GARLIC CLOVES (MINCED)

½ CUP PECORINO ROMANO CHEESE (GRATED)

1 TABLESPOON SALT

¾ TABLESPOON BLACK PEPPER

¼ CUP FRESH PARSLEY (CHOPPED)

4 CUPS VEGETABLE OIL


SOAK BREAD IN WATER, ENOUGH TO DAMPEN FOR 2 HOURS.

DRAIN BREAD OF ANY EXCESS WATER. IN LARGE BOWL, MIX ALL INGREDIENTS TOGETHER WITH FINGERS, MAKING SURE EVERYTHING IS MIXED VERY WELL.

START TO ROLL INTO MEATBALLS A LITTLE BIGGER THAN THE SIZE OF A GOLF BALL. YOU SHOULD GET ABOUT 12 TO 15 MEATBALLS.

ADD 4 CUPS OF OIL TO MEDIUM SIZE FRY PAN. HEAT OIL ON MEDIUM FLAME. WHEN OIL IS HOT, ADD 6 OR 7 MEATBALLS TO PAN (MAKE SURE THERE IS ROOM BETWEEN MEATBALLS FOR EVEN COOKING). COOK ON EACH SIDE FOR ABOUT 3 MINUTES. PLACE MEATBALLS ON BROWN PAPER BAG TO DRAIN OFF OIL.

# PASTA WITH CRABMEAT

¾ POUND FRESH CRABMEAT

6 CUPS MARINARA SAUCE (SEE RECIPE PG. 176)

1 LB. PASTA OF CHOICE (SEE RECIPE PG. 108)


ADD CRABMEAT TO MARINARA SAUCE IN SAUCE POT. BRING TO A BOIL, LOWER FLAME, AND SIMMER FOR 8 MINUTES, STIRRING CONSTANTLY. SERVE ON TOP OF YOUR PASTA OF CHOICE.

SERVES 4 TO 6.


## *THINGS OF INTEREST*

Two South Philadelphians have been elected Mayor of the City of Philadelphia. Can you name them?

The first is easy—Frank Rizzo. Everyone knows about Frank Rizzo. The other one was Bernard "Barney" Samuel, the last Republican Mayor this city has had—and he served 50 years ago! Samuel also served as President of Philadelphia's City Council.

## PASTA WITH GARLIC AND OLIVE OIL

12 LARGE GARLIC CLOVES (MINCED)

4 CUPS EXTRA VIRGIN OLIVE OIL

1 TABLESPOON SALT

¾ TABLESPOON BLACK PEPPER

¾ TABLESPOON OREGANO

¼ CUP FRESH PARSLEY (CHOPPED)

1 LB. PASTA OF CHOICE (SEE RECIPE PG. 108)


SAUTÉ GARLIC, SALT, BLACK PEPPER, OREGANO, AND OLIVE OIL IN LARGE FRY PAN UNTIL GARLIC IS GOLDEN IN COLOR. SERVE ON YOUR PASTA OF CHOICE. GARNISH WITH FRESH PARSLEY.

SERVES 4 TO 6.

## PASTA WITH MUSHROOMS

8 LARGE WHITE MUSHROOMS (SLICED)
6 CUPS MARINARA SAUCE (SEE RECIPE PG. 176)
1 LB. PASTA OF CHOICE (SEE RECIPE PG. 108)

ADD MUSHROOMS TO MARINARA SAUCE IN SAUCEPOT AND BRING TO A BOIL. LOWER FLAME AND SIMMER FOR 10 MINUTES, STIRRING CONSTANTLY. SERVE ON TOP OF YOUR PASTA OF CHOICE.
   SERVES 4 TO 6.

## *WHAT THEY MEAN*

**Fegatini di Pollo** - (feh-gah-TEE-nee dee POHL-loh) means chicken livers.
**Cassata** - (ka-SAH-ta) is an ice cream dish made of a hard shell of cream or chocolate enclosing lighter ice cream. Similar to **Tartuffo** (tar-TOOF-oh).
**Dolce** - (DOHL-cheh) means sweet.

# PASTA WITH SAUSAGE

1 ½ LB. SWEET ITALIAN SAUSAGE

4 CUPS VEGETABLE OIL

6 CUPS MARINARA SAUCE (SEE RECIPE PG. 176)

1 LB. PASTA OF CHOICE (SEE RECIPE PG. 108)

CUT SAUSAGE INTO 1-INCH PIECES. PAN FRY SAUSAGE IN OIL ON MEDIUM HEAT FOR ABOUT 5 MINUTES. TAKE SAUSAGE OUT OF PAN AND ADD TO MARINARA SAUCE IN SAUCEPOT. BRING TO A BOIL, LOWER FLAME, AND SIMMER FOR 8 MINUTES, STIRRING CONSTANTLY. SERVE ON TOP OF YOUR PASTA OF CHOICE.

SERVES 4 TO 6.

# PASTA WITH SHRIMP

16 LARGE SHRIMP (SHELLS OFF AND CLEANED)
6 CUPS MARINARA SAUCE (SEE RECIPE PG. 176)
1 LB. PASTA OF CHOICE (SEE RECIPE PG. 108)

CUT EACH SHRIMP INTO 4 PIECES. ADD TO MARINARA SAUCE IN SAUCEPOT. BRING TO A BOIL, LOWER FLAME, AND SIMMER FOR 10 MINUTES, STIRRING CONSTANTLY. SERVE ON TOP OF YOUR PASTA OF CHOICE.
SERVES 4 TO 6.

## *DID YOU KNOW???*

Did you know that the Italians net some 700 million pounds of fish a year, among them, the "scampi" a close relative of the shrimp that has no exact equivalent outside of Italian waters?

# POTATO GNOCCHI WITH TOMATO SAUCE

1 LB. POTATOES

4 QTS. WATER

1 ¾ CUPS UNBLEACHED FLOUR

2 TABLESPOONS SALT

1 TEASPOON BLACK PEPPER

6 CUPS TOMATO SAUCE (SEE RECIPE PG. 179)

QUARTER THE POTATOES AND BRING TO A BOIL WITH 4 QTS. WATER. WHEN POTATOES ARE TENDER (NOT MUSHY), DRAIN THOROUGHLY IN COLANDER AND MASH WELL. PLACE FLOUR IN A MOUND ON A PASTA BOARD. ADD 1 TABLESPOON SALT AND 1 TEA-SPOON BLACK PEPPER, AND START INCORPORATING POTATOES INTO FLOUR UNTIL DOUGH IS MIXED EVENLY, LEAVING A LITTLE FLOUR ON PASTA BOARD.

CUT DOUGH INTO SEVERAL PIECES AND ROLL EACH PIECE INTO A LONG ROLL, 1 INCH IN DIAMETER. CUT ROLLS INTO ¾ INCH LONG PIECES. TAKE A FORK, PLACE IT ON EACH PIECE, AND ROLL GNOCCHI TOWARDS YOU. THIS WILL CURL GNOCCHI INTO A "C". CON-TINUE THIS UNTIL ALL GNOCCHI ARE DONE. PUT GNOCCHI IN LARGE POT WITH 4 QTS. BOILING WATER AND 1 TABLESPOON SALT, STIRRING TO MAKE SURE GNOCCHI DOESNT STICK. ONCE WATER COMES BACK

TO A BOIL, COOK GNOCCHI FOR 7 MINUTES. WHEN
GNOCCHI ARE DONE, DRAIN WELL IN COLANDER.

WHILE GNOCCHI ARE BOILING, HEAT UP YOUR TO-
MATO SAUCE AND TIME IT SO GNOCCHI ARE DONE
WHEN TOMATO SAUCE IS DONE. SERVE ON GNOCCHI.

SERVES 4 TO 6.

## *DID YOU KNOW???*

Italy is Europe's largest producer of Rice—and the average of Rice-
per-acre, 530 bushels—is unmatched anywhere in the world. Rice
was first known in Italy as early as the 12th Century but was not
cultivated there until four centuries later. At one point in the 18th
Century, it was illegal to take seed grain out of Italy. Some was
smuggled out, ironically, by Thomas Jefferson, who then grew it
successfully in Virginia.

# SPAGHETTI WITH MEATBALLS

". . . I guess it's a bit ironic that 'spaghetti and meatballs' have become almost an American dish because so many people love this meal . . . it is simple and easy to prepare . . . and it is soooo good . . . the origin of this dish is from my ancestors' home region of Naples . . ."

8 MEATBALLS (SEE RECIPE PG. 114)

6 CUPS MARINARA SAUCE (SEE RECIPE PG. 176)

1 LB. SPAGHETTI (SEE PASTA RECIPE PG. 108)


BRING MARINARA SAUCE AND MEATBALLS TO A BOIL IN A LARGE POT, LOWER FLAME, AND SIMMER FOR 15 MINUTES, STIRRING FROM TIME TO TIME (MAKE SURE NOT TO BREAK UP MEATBALLS). SERVE ON SPAGHETTI.

SERVES 4 TO 6.

# ZITI WITH PROSCIUTTO AND PEAS

16 THIN SLICES PROSCIUTTO 3IN./2IN.

¼ LB. BUTTER

1 CUP FROZEN PEAS

4 CUPS ALFREDO SAUCE (SEE RECIPE PG. 174)

2 TABLESPOONS COOKED GARLIC (SEE RECIPE PG. 93)

1 LB. ZITI (SEE RECIPE PG. 108)

¼ CUP FRESH PARSLEY (CHOPPED)

IN LARGE FRYING PAN, SAUTÉ PROSCIUTTO WITH BUTTER FOR 1 MINUTE ON MEDIUM FLAME. ADD PEAS AND CONTINUE TO SAUTÉ FOR 2 MORE MINUTES. AT THIS POINT, ADD ALFREDO SAUCE AND GARLIC, AND SAUTÉ FOR 3 MINUTES (TIME YOUR SAUCE SO WHEN PASTA IS DONE, SAUCE WILL BE DONE ALSO). TOSS IN YOUR ZITI AND SERVE TOPPED WITH FRESH PARSLEY. SERVES 4.

# CHAPTER 10

## *Seafood Dishes*

*Next to Pasta, the sea is the source of Italy's most important source of food. In fact, most Italian provinces have seacoasts and each has created its own special, delicious recipes.*

## BACCALA (SALTED CODFISH)

". . . This fish is traditionally served as one of the seven fishes on Christmas Eve, but it really can be eaten and enjoyed any time of the year."

5 LBS. DRY, SALTED BACCALA

5 CUPS MARINARA SAUCE

2 LARGE SPANISH ONIONS (SLICED)

20 PITTED BLACK OLIVES (SLICED)

2 TABLESPOONS CAPERS

SOAK FISH IN COLD WATER FOR 1 TO 2 DAYS, CHANGING WATER FREQUENTLY. DRAIN WATER AND PAT DRY. SLICE FISH INTO 8-10 OZ. PIECES.

PLACE FISH AND REMAINING INGREDIENTS IN A 12 X 14 INCH BAKING PAN, BAKE IN PREHEATED OVEN SET AT 350 DEGREES FOR 35 MINUTES.

SERVES 8.

# CHILEAN SEA BASS SICILIAN

4 PIECES CHILIAN SEA BASS (ABOUT 12 OZS. EACH)

4 CUPS MARINARA SAUCE (SEE RECIPE PG. 176)

1 LARGE SPANISH ONION (SLICED THIN)

16 BLACK OLIVES (SLICED THIN)

2 TABLESPOONS COOKED GARLIC (SEE RECIPE PG. 93)

½ CUP RED WINE VINEGAR

2 TABLESPOONS WORCESTERSHIRE SAUCE

2 TABLESPOONS TABASCO SAUCE

IN LARGE FRYING PAN, ADD FISH AND ALL INGRE-DIENTS. BRING TO A BOIL, LOWER FLAME, AND SIMMER FOR 10-12 MINUTES.

SERVES 4.

## *THINGS OF INTEREST*

The Tuscany and Piedmont regions are the largest producers of wine in Italy.

# FLOUNDER FRANCAISE

4 –10 OZ. PIECES FRESH FLOUNDER

3 CUPS FLOUR

6 EGGS (BEATEN)

4 CUPS VEGETABLE OIL

½ POUND BUTTER

½ CUP HEAVY CREAM

2 LEMONS (CUT IN HALF, SEEDS REMOVED)

4 TABLESPOONS RUE (SEE RECIPE PG. 94)

2 TABLESPOONS COOKED GARLIC (SEE RECIPE PG. 93)

½ TEASPOON BLACK PEPPER

½ TEASPOON OREGANO

½ TEASPOON TARRAGON


DREDGE FLOUNDER IN FLOUR, DIP IN EGG, AND LET SOAK FOR 10 MINUTES. ADD OIL TO LARGE FRY PAN ON MEDIUM HEAT. WHEN OIL IS HOT, ADD FISH AND SAUTÉ FOR 2 MINUTES ON EACH SIDE. DRAIN OIL AND ADD REMAINING INGREDIENTS. BRING TO A BOIL AND SIMMER ON LOW FLAME FOR 4 MINUTES, STIRRING CONSTANTLY.

PLACE 1 PIECE OF FLOUNDER ON EACH PLATE. PUT PAN BACK ON STOVE AND WHIP. SPOON SAUCE ON FLOUNDER.

SERVES 4.

# MONKFISH FRA DIAVOLO

". . . This fish is known as a 'poor man's lobster' because its' texture and flavor are similar to lobster . . ."

4 PIECES MONKFISH (ABOUT 12 OZS. EACH)

4 CUPS MARINARA SAUCE (SEE RECIPE PG. 176)

2 TABLESPOONS COOKED GARLIC (SEE RECIPE PG. 93)

¼ CUP SAUTERNE WINE

2 TABLESPOONS TABASCO SAUCE

2 TABLESPOONS WORCESTERSHIRE SAUCE

1 TEASPOON BLACK PEPPER

1 TEASPOON OREGANO


WASH MONKFISH, AND TRIM MEMBRANE FROM FISH. ADD FISH AND ALL INGREDIENTS TO LARGE FRYING PAN. BRING TO A BOIL, LOWER FLAME, AND SIMMER FOR 12 MINUTES.

SERVES 4.


## *THINGS OF INTEREST*

The most famous example of the Neapolitan style of cooking is pizza, which grew to be so popular in the United States that it had to be re-introduced in Naples, where the locals had lost interest in it—mostly to be consumed by tourists.

## POACHED RAINBOW TROUT

4-1LB. TROUT (FILETED)

½ LB. BUTTER

4 TABLESPOONS RUE (SEE RECIPE PG. 94)

2 TABLESPOONS COOKED GARLIC (SEE RECIPE PG. 93)

2 LEMONS (CUT IN HALF, SEEDS REMOVED)

½ TEASPOON BLACK PEPPER


SAUTÉ TROUT, SKIN DOWN, IN LARGE FRY PAN WITH ALL INGREDIENTS ON MEDIUM FLAME FOR 8 MINUTES. (DO NOT FLIP TROUT. IT WILL COOK ON BOTH SIDES WITH SKIN DOWN). STIR CONSTANTLY. SERVE TROUT ON SERVING PLATE. PUT PAN BACK ON STOVE, BRING BACK TO A BOIL, AND WHIP ALL INGREDIENTS. SPOON ON TROUT.

SERVES 4.

# SHRIMP MARINARA

"... This dish can also be served on pasta ..."

24 LARGE SHRIMP (SHELLS OFF AND CLEANED)
6 CUPS MARINARA SAUCE (SEE RECIPE PG. 176)

AFTER PEELING AND CLEANING SHRIMP, SAUTÉ
IN MEDIUM SAUCE POT WITH MARINARA SAUCE.
BRING TO A BOIL, LOWER FLAME, AND SIMMER FOR
8 MINUTES.
SERVES 4 TO 6.

## *THINGS OF INTEREST*

Napoleon was exiled to Elba and stayed there for 10 months before returning home to be defeated at Waterloo. Elba is an Island
in the Italian district of Livorno. They say that fish are so abun-
dant for the residents of Elba that the only way they would consider buying it is still alive.

# SHRIMP SCAMPI

". . . This scampi recipe is the traditional way to make it. You will also see this made with garlic and oil in some restaurants, which is also very good. This dish can also be served on pasta . . ."

24 LARGE SHRIMP (SHELLS OFF AND CLEANED)

1 LB. BUTTER

¼ CUP RUE (SEE RECIPE PG. 94)

¼ CUP SAUTERNE WINE

½ CUP HEAVY CREAM

¾ TEASPOON WHITE PEPPER

6 LARGE GARLIC CLOVES (MINCED)

2 LEMONS (CUT IN HALF, SEEDS REMOVED)

FRESH PARSLEY, ENOUGH TO GARNISH (CHOPPED)

SAUTÉ SHRIMP IN LARGE FRY PAN ON MEDIUM FLAME WITH ALL INGREDIENTS EXCEPT PARSLEY (MAKE SURE NOT TO BURN BUTTER), STIRRING CONSTANTLY. SAUTÉ FOR 8 MINUTES. SERVE AND GARNISH WITH PARSLEY.

# CHAPTER 11

## *Meats (Pork Chops, Veal Chops, And Steak)*

*The Dispigno family came to the United States from Naples in 1893. What the world knows as "Italian Cooking" originated in the creative hands and minds of Neapolitans who took their native cooking to the lands to which they emigrated . . . and from which we have all benefited.*

## BROILED PORK CHOPS WITH BURNT ONIONS

8 – 6 OZ. CENTER CUT PORK CHOPS

2 LARGE SPANISH ONIONS (SLICED)

½ CUP VEGETABLE OIL

1 TABLESPOON BUTTER

¼ CUP SAUTERNE WINE

1 TEASPOON SALT

½ TEASPOON BLACK PEPPER

½ TEASPOON OREGANO

1 TABLESPOON COOKED GARLIC (SEE RECIPE PG. 93)

FRESH PARSLEY, ENOUGH TO GARNISH (CHOPPED)

BROIL PORK CHOPS. WHILE CHOPS ARE BROILING, SAUTÉ ONIONS WITH OIL AND BUTTER IN MEDIUM FRY PAN. COOK ONIONS UNTIL THEY ARE BROWNED ALMOST TO THE POINT OF BEING BURNT. AT THIS POINT, DEGLAZE PAN WITH SAUTERNE AND ADD RE-MAINING INGREDIENTS. SAUTÉ FOR 3 MINUTES. WHEN CHOPS ARE DONE, TOP WITH ONIONS. GAR-NISH WITH PARSLEY.

SERVES 4 TO 6.

## *DID YOU KNOW???*

Most Italians prefer veal to beef—it is a trait carried over from the Ancient Romans. There is a division, however, about veal in Italy. North of Florence, veal is *vitello* (or calf). South of Florence, veal is *vitella* (or heifer). In the north, the cows are reared solely for milk production and only the steers are killed for meat. In the south, cattle are not great milk producers and they are raised primarily for field work.

# BROILED VEAL CHOP WITH GARLIC AND OIL

". . . I love to watch our customers when they are done eating the meat off the chop, pick it up, and start eating off the bone. This is really the only way to eat a veal chop . . .".

4 –16 OZ. MILK FED LION VEAL CHOPS

8 TABLESPOONS OF COOKED GARLIC WITH OIL (SEE RECIPE PG. 93)

FRESH PARSLEY, ENOUGH TO GARNISH (CHOPPED)

BROIL VEAL CHOPS UNTIL MEDIUM (OR WHATEVER YOUR PREFRANCE).

WHEN CHOPS ARE DONE, PUT ON SERVING PLATE AND TOP WITH COOKED GARLIC AND OIL. GARNISH WITH PARSLEY.

SERVES 4.

## *THINGS OF INTEREST*

South Philadelphia was the birthplace of several major league baseball players, including Al Brancato (Philadelphia A's), Eddie Silber (St. Louis Browns), Adam Swigler (New York Giants), George Riley (Cubs, Giants, Expos), Frank DiMichele (California Angels), Harry Marnie (Phillies), and John Marzano (Boston Red Sox).
A's Manager Connie Mack (1901-50) was a frequent visitor to Ralph's.

# BROILED VEAL CHOP WITH MUSHROOMS AND PEPPERS

4 –16 OZ. MILK FED LOIN VEAL CHOPS

2 LARGE RED BELL PEPPERS (SLICED)

8 LARGE WHITE MUSHROOMS (SLICED)

½ CUP VEGETABLE OIL

¼ CUP SAUTERNE WINE

½ TEASPOON SALT

¼ TEASPOON BLACK PEPPER

¼ TEASPOON OREGANO

2 TABLESPOONS COOKED GARLIC (SEE RECIPE PG. 93)

FRESH PARSLEY, ENOUGH TO GARNISH (CHOPPED)


BROIL VEAL CHOPS TO MEDIUM. WHILE VEAL CHOPS ARE BROILING, SAUTE PEPPERS AND MUSH-ROOMS WITH ALL INGREDIENTS EXCEPT GARLIC AND PAESLEY FOR 3 MINUTES. AT THIS POINT ADD GARLIC AND PARSLEY AND SAUTE FOR 1 MINUTE. WHEN VEAL CHOPS ARE COOKED TOP WITH MUSHROOMS AND PEPPERS.

SERVES 4.

# PORK CHOPS PIZZAIOLA

8 - 6OZ. CENTER CUT PORK CHOPS

6 CUPS MARINARA SAUCE (SEE RECIPE PG. 176)

¼ CUP SAUTERNE WINE

2 TABLESPOONS WORCESTERSHIRE SAUCE

1 TEASPOON OREGANO

½ TEASPOON BLACK PEPPER

FRESH PARSLEY, ENOUGH TO GARNISH (CHOPPED)

BROIL PORK CHOPS UNTIL ALMOST COOKED. WHILE PORK CHOPS ARE BROILING, PUT ALL INGREDIENTS IN LARGE FRY PAN. MIX WELL. WHEN CHOPS ARE ALMOST COOKED, ADD TO PAN. BRING TO A BOIL, LOWER FLAME, AND SIMMER FOR 6 MINUTES, TURNING CHOPS SO BOTH SIDES COOK. SERVE AND GARNISH WITH PARSLEY.

SERVES 4 TO 6.

# STEAK FRA DIAVOLO

"... This dish can also have mozzarella or provolone cheese melted over it ..."

4-16 OZ. SIRLION STEAKS

6 CUPS MARINARA SAUCE (SEE RECIPE PG. 176)

½ CUP SAUTERNE WINE

1 TEASPOON RED PEPPER (CRUSHED)

1 TEASPOON BLACK PEPPER

1 TEASPOON OREGANO

2 TABLESPOONS WORCESTERSHIRE SAUCE

2 TABLESPOONS TABASCO SAUCE

¼ CUP FRESH PARSLEY (CHOPPED)


BROIL STEAKS TO YOUR LIKING. WHILE STEAKS ARE BROILING, ADD REMAINING INGREDIENTS TO LARGE FRY PAN (EXCEPT PARSLEY).

DO NOT PUT BACK ON FLAME UNTIL STEAKS ARE ADDED. WHEN STEAKS ARE DONE, ADD TO PAN. BRING TO A BOIL, LOWER FLAME, AND SIMMER FOR 5 MIN-UTES, STIRRING CONSTANTLY. SERVE AND TOP WITH PARSLEY.

SERVES 4.

# CHAPTER 12

## *Poultry*

*No Italian market—old world or new—would be complete without a full array of poultry. The Italians love to cook poultry—ducks and geese, chickens from their native land, and once they came to America, the turkey—there are countless delicious ways to cook poultry. Here are a few of our favorites.*

## BROILED CHICKEN

"... When the chicken is finished, the skin will have a burnt look to it. Don't panic, that means you cooked it the way it is supposed to be. If you'd rather not eat the skin, the chicken can also be cooked without it ..."

1-3LB. CHICKEN

¼ CUP OLIVE OIL

6 LARGE WHITE MUSHROOMS (SLICED)

1 TABLESPOON BUTTER

SALT (PINCH)

BLACK PEPPER (PINCH)

OREGANO (PINCH)

1 TEASPOON COOKED GARLIC (SEE RECIPE PG. 93)

2 TABLESPOONS FRESH PARSLEY (CHOPPED)

WASH CHICKEN THOROUGHLY AND SLICE IN HALF. THEN, QUARTER EACH HALF (*EXAMPLE*: SEPARATE WING, LEG, THIGH, BREAST). PLACE IN BROILER, TURNING OCCASIONALLY TO MAKE SURE BOTH SIDES COOK.

WHILE CHICKEN IS BROILING, SAUTÉ MUSHROOMS WITH OLIVE OIL, BUTTER, SALT, BLACK PEPPER, AND OREGANO FOR 4 MINUTES IN A MEDIUM FRY PAN. AT THIS POINT, ADD GARLIC AND SAUTÉ FOR 1 MORE MINUTE. WHEN CHICKEN IS DONE, TOP WITH SAUTÉED MUSHROOMS AND GARNISH WITH FRESH PARSLEY.

SERVES 2 TO 3.

## *DID YOU KNOW???*

Two-time Heavyweight Boxing Champion of the World (during the 1980's) Tim Witherspoon, was born in South Philadelphia and is a graduate of South Philadelphia High School.

# CHICKEN CACCIATORE

"... This is a meal fit for a King and is one of my favorites. When the chicken is done the meat falls off the bone ..."

1-3LB. CHICKEN

4 CUPS MARINARA SAUCE (SEE RECIPE PG. 176)

3 CUPS VEGETABLE OIL

¼ CUP SAUTERNE WINE

¼ SHERRY WINE

½ CUP WATER

3 LARGE GREEN BELL PEPPERS (SLICED)

6 LARGE WHITE MUSHROOMS (SLICED)

1 LARGE SPANISH ONION (SLICED)

1 TEASPOON ROSEMARY

SALT (PINCH)

BLACK PEPPER (PINCH)

1/8 CUP FRESH BASIL (CHOPPED)

IF FRESH BASIL ISN'T AVAILABLE, USE A PINCH OF DRY

1/8 CUP FRESH PARSLEY (CHOPPED)


WASH CHICKEN THOROUGHLY AND SLICE IN HALF. THEN, QUARTER EACH HALF (EXAMPLE: SEPARATE WING, LEG, THIGH, AND BREAST). PAN FRY CHICKEN WITH OIL IN LARGE FRY PAN FOR 6 MINUTES, UNTIL SKIN IS CRISPY. PLACE CHICKEN IN 4 QT. POT WITH REMAINING INGREDIENTS AND BRING TO A BOIL. LOWER FLAME AND SIMMER FOR 20 MINUTES, STIRRING CONSTANTLY.

SERVES 4 TO 6.

# CHICKEN CUTLETS

8 EGGS

4 CUPS BREAD CRUMBS

4 CUPS FLOUR

8 CHICKEN BREASTS

3 CUPS VEGETABLE OIL

BEAT EGGS IN LARGE BOWL. PUT BREAD CRUMBS AND FLOUR IN SEPARATE BOWLS LARGE ENOUGH TO DIP CHICKEN BREASTS. DIP CHICKEN IN FLOUR, THEN EGG WASH, AND THEN BREAD CRUMBS. REPEAT THIS PROCESS TWICE. SAUTÉ CHICKEN WITH OIL IN LARGE FRY PAN ON MEDIUM FLAME, 3 MINUTES ON EACH SIDE. PLACE CHICKEN ON PAPER TOWELS TO DRAIN OIL.

SERVES 4 TO 6.

# CHICKEN PARMIGIANA

4 CUPS MARINARA SAUCE (SEE RECIPE PG. 176)

24 SLICES MOZZARELLA

FOLLOW CHICKEN CUTLET RECIPE. WHEN CUTLETS ARE DONE, COAT LARGE BAKING PAN (BIG ENOUGH TO FIT 8 CHICKEN BREASTS) WITH 3 CUPS MARINARA SAUCE. PLACE CHICKEN IN PAN AND LAYER WITH 3 PIECES OF MOZZARELLA ON EACH. TOP WITH REMAINING SAUCE. BAKE IN PREHEATED OVEN AT 375 DEGREES FOR 25 MINUTES.

## *THINGS OF INTEREST*

The Emperor Maximus of Rome (235-238 AD) is said to have eaten 40 pounds of meat daily and washed it down with 40 quarts of wine. In ancient Rome, elephant trunk was considered a delicacy, along with camel's feet and donkey meat. To impress Emperor Aurelian, an actor named Farone was reputed to have consumed a whole sheep, a suckling pig, and a wild boar, along with 100 buns and 100 bottles of wine at one sitting. Pass the Tums, please!

# CHICKEN SORRENTO

"... This is one of the most popular dishes at Ralph's. Enough said! ..."

3 CUPS FLOUR

8 BONELESS CHICKEN BREASTS

2 CUPS VEGETABLE OIL

½ LB. BUTTER

3 TABLESPOONS RUE (SEE RECIPE PG. 94)

½ CUP SHERRY WINE

24 SLICES MOZZARELLA (SLICED THIN)

DREDGE CHICKEN BREAST IN FLOUR. SAUTÉ CHICKEN BREASTS WITH OIL IN LARGE FRYING PAN, 3 MINUTES ON EACH SIDE. DRAIN OIL OUT OF PAN. ADD BUTTER, RUE, AND WINE. BRING TO A BOIL, LOWER FLAME, AND SIMMER FOR 4 MINUTES, STIRRING CONSTANTLY. AT THIS POINT, LAYER 3 PIECES OF MOZZARELLA ON EACH CHICKEN BREAST AND PUT PAN IN BROILER UNTIL CHEESE IS MELTED (ABOUT 1 MINUTE). SERVE 2 CHICKEN BREASTS ON EACH PLATE. PUT PAN BACK ON STOVE. BRING TO A BOIL, WHIP SAUCE, AND SPOON ON CHICKEN.

SERVES 4 TO 6.

# CHAPTER 13

## *Veal*

*Like their ancient Roman ancestors, most Italians prefer veal to beef. North of Florence, veal is vitello (calf) and south of Florence, it is vitella (heifer). Whatever you call it and whatever your ancestry, veal makes a wonderful dish.*

## VEAL CAPRICCIOSA

1 LARGE SPANISH ONION (CHOPPED)

6 CUPS VEGETABLE OIL

1-28 OZ. CAN TOMATOES (CRUSHED BY HAND)

1 TALBESPOON SALT

1 TEASPOON BLACK PEPPER

2 LARGE EGGPLANT (PEELED)

4 CUPS FLOUR

8 EGGS (BEATEN)

12-2 OZ. MILK FED VEAL MEDALLIONS

¼ CUP PECORINO ROMANO CHEESE (GRATED)

12 THIN SLICES PROSCIUTTO (3 IN. X 2 IN.)

24 SLICES MOZZARELLA CHEESE (SLICED 1/8 IN. THICK)

½ CUP SAUTERNE WINE

¼ CUP FRESH PARSLEY (CHOPPED)

SAUTE ONION IN 1 CUP VEGETABLE OIL UNTIL GOLDEN COLOR.ADD TOMATOES, SALT, AND BLACK PEPPER TO 4 QT. POT.BRING TO A BOIL,LOWER FLAME AND SIMMER FOR 45 MINUTES.

WHILE SAUCE IS COOKING,SLICE EGGPLANT INTO ¼ IN. SLICES.DIP IN FLOUR,THEN BEATEN EGGS AND SAUTE IN 3 CUPS VEGETABLE OIL ON BOTH SIDES FOR 2 MINUTES EACH, UNTIL ALL EGGPLANT ARE COOKED.PLACE EGGPLANT ON PAPER TOWLES TO DRAIN OFF OIL.

DIP VEAL IN FLOUR, AND SAUTE IN 2 CUPS OF VEG-ETABLE OIL ON BOTH SIDES FOR 2 MINUTES EACH.PLACE VEAL ON PAPER TOWLES TO DRAIN OFF OIL.

COAT BOTTOM OF LARGE FRYING PAN WITH 1 CUP OF SAUCE.ADD VEAL AND LAYER EACH PIECE WITH 1 PIECE OF EGGPLANT, 1 PIECE OF PROSCIUTTO, AND 2 PIECES OF MOZARELLA.TOP WITH REMAINING SAUCE AND SAUTERNE WINE AND BAKE IN PREHEATED OVEN AT 375 DEGREES FOR 45 MINUTES.

SERVE 3 PIECES OF VEAL ON EACH PLATE AND GAR-NISH WITH FRESH PARSLEY.

SERVES 4 TO 6.

# VEAL CACCIATORE

1 LARGE SPANISH ONION (SLICED)

1 CUP OLIVE OIL

3 LBS. VEAL CUBES (1 INCH CUBES, STEWING VEAL)

4 CUPS MARINARA SAUCE (SEE RECIPE PG. 176)

1 CUP WATER

½ CUP SAUTERNE WINE

3 LARGE GREEN BELL PEPPERS (SLICED)

6 LARGE WHITE MUSHROOMS (SLICED)

1 TABLESPOON ROSEMARY

1 TEASPOON SALT

1 TEASPOON BLACK PEPPER

1 TEASPOON OREGANO

¼ CUP FRESH BASIL (CHOPPED)

IF FRESH IS NOT AVAILABLE, USE 1 TEASPOON DRY

¼ CUP FRESH PARSLEY (CHOPPED)


SAUTÉ ONION WITH OLIVE OIL IN 4 QT. POT. WHEN ONION IS TRANSPARENT, ADD VEAL, MARINARA SAUCE, AND WATER. BRING TO A BOIL, LOWER FLAME, AND SIMMER VEAL FOR 15 MINUTES. AT THIS POINT, ADD REMAINING INGREDIENTS AND SIMMER FOR A HALF HOUR, OR UNTIL VEAL IS TENDER, STIRRING CONSTANTLY.

SERVES 4.

# VEAL ALFRESCA

6-2 OZ. MEDALLIONS OF MILK FED VEAL (POUNDED THIN)
8 GARLIC CLOVES
½ CUP ROASTED PEPPERS (SLICED)
6 ARTICHOKE HEARTS (QUARTERED)
1CUP OLIVE OIL
1 CUP FLOUR
¼ CUP SAUTERNE WATER
PINCH SALT
PINCH BLACK PEPPER
6 FRESH BASIL LEAVES (CHOPPED)

SAUTÉ GARLIC CLOVES WITH 1/2-CUP OLIVE OIL IN SMALL FRY PAN ON MEDIUM FLAME, UNTIL GOLDEN IN COLOR. DRAIN OIL, SET ASIDE.

DREDGE VEAL IN FLOUR. SAUTÉ IN NON-STICK FRY PAN WITH 3/4 CUP OF OLIVE OIL (RESERVE 1/4 CUP FOR DISHOUT) 2 MINUTES ON EACH SIDE.

DRAIN PAN OF OIL.

AT THIS POINT, ADD WINE, 1/4 CUP OLIVE OIL, GAR-LIC CLOVES, ARTICHOKE HEARTS, ROASTED PEPPER, SEASONINGS, AND FRESH BASIL. SAUTÉ ALL INGREDI-ENTS TOGETHER FOR 3 MINUTES ON MEDIUM FLAME, MAKING SURE THAT NOTHING STICKS TO THE BOT-TOM OF THE PAN.

SERVES 2.

# VEAL CUTLETS

4-4OZ. MEDALLIONS MILK FED VEAL (POUNDED THIN)
8 EGGS
4 CUPS BREAD CRUMBS
4 CUPS FLOUR
3 CUPS VEGETABLE OIL
2 LEMONS (QUARTERED)

BEAT EGGS IN MEDIUM BOWL. SPREAD BREAD CRUMBS IN FLAT 12 INCH BAKING PAN. SPREAD FLOUR IN SEPARATE 12 INCH BAKING PAN. DIP CUTLETS IN FLOUR, EGG WASH, BREAD CRUMBS, THEN EGG WASH AND BREAD CRUMBS AGAIN. (ONE AT A TIME)

PAN FRY CUTLETS WITH OIL (1 AT A TIME) IN LARGE NON-STICK FRYING PAN, 2 MINUTES ON EACH SIDE, MAKING SURE OIL IS HOT FIRST. AS CUTLETS ARE DONE, LAY ON PAPER TOWELS TO DRAIN OIL. SERVE WITH 2 LEMON WEDGES EACH.

SERVES 4.

# VEAL PARMIGIANA

4 CUPS MARINARA SAUCE (SEE RECIPE PG. 176)
16 SLICES MOZZARELLA (SLICED THIN)

FOLLOW VEAL CUTLET RECIPE (EXCLUDING LEMONS). WHEN CUTLETS ARE DONE, COAT A BAKING PAN (LARGE ENOUGH TO FIT ALL 4 CUTLETS) WITH ABOUT HALF THE MARINARA SAUCE. PLACE CUTLETS IN PAN AND LAYER 4 SLICES OF MOZZARELLA ON EACH CUTLET. POUR REMAINING MARINARA SAUCE ON EACH CUTLET, AND BAKE IN PREHEATED OVEN AT 400 DEGREES FOR 25 MINUTES.

## *WHAT IT IS*

**Broccoli Rabe** - Broccoli Rabe is a pungent, bitter green that's not as popular in America as it is in Italy, where it's often sautéed, braised, or steamed, as well as used in soups and salads. It's available in many markets in both the fall and spring and is a favorite at Ralph's.

# VEAL FRANCAISE

12-2 OZ. MEDALLIONS MILK FED VEAL (POUNDED THIN)
2 CUPS FLOUR
4 EGGS (BEATEN)
2 CUPS VEGETABLE OIL
½ LB. BUTTER
3 TABLESPOONS RUE (SEE RECIPE PG. 94)
½ CUP SHERRY WINE
2 LEMONS (CUT IN HALF, SEEDS REMOVED)

DREDGE VEAL MEDALLIONS IN FLOUR, THEN DIP IN EGG WASH.

SAUTÉ VEAL WITH OIL IN LARGE NON-STICK FRY PAN, 2 MINUTES ON EACH SIDE (MAKE SURE OIL IS HOT.) WHEN VEAL IS DONE, DRAIN OIL OUT OF PAN. ADD REMAINING INGREDIENTS AND SQUEEZE IN LEMON JUICE. BRING TO A BOIL, LOWER FLAME, AND SIMMER FOR 2 MINUTES.

SERVES 4.

# VEAL MOZZARELLA

12-2 OZ. MEDALLIONS MILK FED VEAL (POUNDED THIN)
2 CUPS FLOUR
2 CUPS VEGETABLE OIL
½ LB. BUTTER
4 TABLESPOONS RUE (SEE RECIPE PG. 94)      ·
¼ CUP SHERRY WINE
24 SLICES MOZZARELLA (SLICED THIN)

DREDGE VEAL IN FLOUR. SAUTÉ VEAL WITH OIL IN LARGE, NON-STICK FRYING PAN FOR 2 MINUTES ON EACH SIDE. WHEN VEAL IS DONE, DRAIN OIL OUT OF PAN. ADD BUTTER, RUE, AND SHERRY. BRING TO A BOIL, LOWER FLAME, AND SIMMER FOR 2 MINUTES, STIRRING CONSTANTLY. AT THIS POINT, LAYER 2 PIECES OF MOZZARELLA ON EACH PIECE OF VEAL. PUT PAN IN BROILER TO MELT CHEESE (ABOUT 1 MINUTE). SERVE 3 PIECES OF VEAL ON EACH PLATE, THEN PUT PAN BACK ON STOVE. BRING TO ABOIL, WHIP SAUCE, AND SPOON ON VEAL.

SERVES 4.

# VEAL PICCANTE

12-2 OZ. MEDALLIONS MILK FED VEAL (POUNDED THIN)

2 CUPS FLOUR

2 CUPS VEGETABLE OIL

½ LB. BUTTER

4 TABLESPOONS RUE (SEE RECIPE PG. 94)

4 LEMONS (CUT IN HALF, SEEDS REMOVED)

2 LEMONS SLICED INTO 12 SLICES (FOR GARNISH)

DREDGE VEAL IN FLOUR. SAUTÉ VEAL WITH OIL IN LARGE, NON-STICK FRYING PAN FOR 2 MINUTESON EACH SIDE. DRAIN OIL OUT OF PAN. ADD BUTTER, RUE, AND SQUEEZE JUICE FROM 4 LEMON HALVES. BRING TO A BOIL, LOWER FLAME, AND SAUTÉ FOR 2 MINUTES, STIRRING CONSTANTLY. SERVE 3 PIECES OF VEAL ON EACH PLATE. WHIP BUTTER IN PAN AND SPOON ON VEAL. GARNISH WITH SLICED LEMONS, 1ON EACH PIECE OF VEAL.

SERVES 4.

# VEAL ROLLATINE

12-2 OZ. MEDALLIONS MILK FED VEAL (POUNDED THIN)

2 CUPS FLOUR

2 CUPS VEGETABLE OIL

1 TABLESPOON BLACK PEPPER

1 TABLESPOON GARLIC POWDER

2 TABLESPOONS PECORINO ROMANO CHEESE (GRATED)

12 SLICES PROSCIUTTO (SLICED 1 INCH WIDE BY 3 INCHES LONG)

12 SLICES MOZZARELLA

8 LARGE WHITE MUSHROOMS (SLICED)

½ LB. BUTTER

4 TABLESPOONS RUE (SEE RECIPE PG. 94)

¼ CUP SHERRY WINE

¼ CUP FRESH PARSLEY (CHOPPED)

DREDGE VEAL IN FLOUR. SAUTÉ VEAL WITH OIL IN LARGE, NON-STICK FRYING PAN FOR 2 MINUTES ON EACH SIDE. WHEN VEAL IS DONE, DRAIN OIL. SEASON VEAL WITH BLACK PEPPER, GARLIC POWDER, AND ROMANO CHEESE. LAYER 1 PIECE OF PROSCIUTTO AND 1 PIECE MOZZARELLA ON EACH MEDALLION. ADD MUSHROOMS, BUTTER, RUE, AND WINE. BRING TO A BOIL AND SAUTÉ ON MEDIUM HEAT FOR 4 MINUTES, STIRRING CONSTANTLY. PLACE 3 PIECES OF VEAL ON EACH PLATE. PUT PAN BACK ON FLAME AND WHIP IN-GREDIENTS TOGETHER UNTIL IT THICKENS. SPOON SAUCE AND MUSHROOMS ON VEAL. GARNISH WITH PARSLEY.

SERVES 4.

# VEAL STEW

1 LARGE SPANISH ONION (SLICED)

1 CUP OLIVE OIL

3 LBS. VEAL CUBES (1 INCH CUBES, STEWING VEAL)

2 LARGE RUSSET POTATOES (PEELED, CUT INTO 1 INCH CUBES)

6 CUPS MARINARA SAUCE (SEE RECIPE PG. 176)

2 CUPS WATER

1 CUP SAUTERNE WINE

1 CUP FROZEN PEAS

6 LARGE WHITE MUSHROOMS (SLICED)

1 TABLESPOON ROSEMARY

1 TEASPOON SALT

1 TEASPOON BLACK PEPPER

1 TEASPOON OREGANO

¼ CUP FRESH BASIL (CHOPPED)

IF FRESH IS NOT AVAILABLE, USE 1 TEASPOON DRY

¼ CUP FRESH PARSLEY (CHOPPED)

SAUTÉ ONION IN OLIVE OIL IN 4 QT. POT. WHEN ONION IS TRANSPARENT, ADD VEAL, POTATOES, MARINARA SAUCE, AND WATER. BRING TO A BOIL, LOWER FLAME, AND SIMMER FOR 15 MINUTES. AT THIS POINT, ADD REMAINING INGREDIENTS AND SIMMER FOR 20 MINUTES, OR UNTIL VEAL AND POTATOES ARE TENDER, STIRRING CONSTANTLY.

SERVES 4.

# VEAL WITH PEPPERS AND MUSHROOMS

12-2 OZ. MEDALLIONS MILK FED VEAL (POUNDED
   THIN)

2 CUPS FLOUR

2 CUPS VEGETABLE OIL

3 MEDIUM GREEN BELL PEPPERS (SLICED)

4 LARGE WHITE MUSHROOMS (SLICED)

6 CUPS MARINARA SAUCE (SEE RECIPE PG. 176)


DREDGE VEAL IN FLOUR. SAUTÉ VEAL WITH OIL IN LARGE, NON-STICK FRYING PAN FOR 2 MINUTES ON EACH SIDE. DRAIN OIL OUT OF PAN, SET PAN ASIDE.

IN 2QT POT, ADD MARINARA SAUCE, PEPPERS, AND MUSHROOMS.

BRING TO A BOIL. LOWER FLAME AND SIMMER FOR 10 MINUTES, STIRRING CONSTANTLY. ADD SAUCE WITH PEPPERS AND MUSHROOMS TO FRYING PAN WITH VEAL, AND BRING BACK TO A BOIL. SERVE.

SERVES 4.

## VEAL WITH VEAL STOCK AND SHITAKI MUSHROOMS

12-2 OZ. MEDALLIONS MILK FED VEAL

2 CUPS FLOUR

2 CUPS VEGETABLE OIL

16 SHITAKI MUSHROOMS (STEMS CUT OFF)

4 CUPS VEAL STOCK (SEE RECIPE PG. 95)

2 TABLESPOONS COOKED GARLIC (SEE RECIPE PG. 93)


DREDGE VEAL IN FLOUR. SAUTÉ VEAL WITH OIL IN A LARGE, NON-STICK FRYING PAN FOR 2 MINUTES ON EACH SIDE. DRAIN OIL. ADD MUSHROOMS, VEAL STOCK, AND GARLIC. SIMMER ON MEDIUM FLAME FOR 3 MINUTES.

SERVES 4.


## *WHAT THEY MEAN . . .*

**Gnocchi** (NYOH-kee) - Italian for "dumplings," gnocchi are small round pasta made from a dough of mashed potatoes.

**Frittata** (free-TAT-ah) - An Italian omelet that's prepared open-faced with the fillings sprinkled on top rather than folded in.

# CHAPTER 14

## Italian Specialties

*The Italian peninsula was the home of the first fully developed cuisine in Europe. Its originators were the ancient Romans, who found their culinary inspiration in Asia Minor and Greece, and combined those inspirations with their own homegrown resources and ingredients. From these roots the Italians have taught the world to cook—and enjoy—fine food. Here are some distinctly Italian dishes.*

## CHICKEN LIVERS WITH MUSHROOMS

". . . When preparing chicken livers, make sure that they are rinsed well and drained of any water. If not, that could prevent them from becoming crispy during the cooking process . . ."

3 LBS. CHICKEN LIVERS (DRAINED)

1 ½ CUPS VEGETABLE OIL

1 LARGE SPANISH ONION (SLICED)

8 LARGE WHITE MUSHROOMS (SLICED)

¾ CUP SAUTERNE WINE

¼ LB BUTTER

4 TABLESPOONS COOKED GARLIC (SEE RECIPE PG. 93)

1 TABLESPOON SALT

1 TEASPOON BLACK PEPPER
1 TEASPOON OREGANO
¼ CUP FRESH PARSLEY (CHOPPED)


SAUTÉ ONION WITH ¼ CUP OIL IN MEDIUM FRY-
ING PAN ON MEDIUM FLAME, UNTIL GOLDEN IN
COLOR. DRAIN ONIONS IN A COLANDER, AND SET
ASIDE. IN A LARGE FRYING PAN, SAUTÉ CHICKEN LIV-
ERS ON HIGH FLAME UNTIL NO LONGER PINK INSIDE,
AND CRISPY OUTSIDE. DRAIN PAN OF OIL AND
DEGLAZE WITH ¾ CUP OF SAUTERNE. ADD MUSH-
ROOMS, ONIONS, AND REMAINING INGREDIENTS,
AND CONTINUE TO SAUTÉ FOR 3 MINUTES ON ME-
DIUM FLAME.

SERVES 4 TO 6.

# EGGPLANT PARMIGIANA

"... This is a great dish for vegetarians who also eat eggs and a dish that is healthy for you ..."

8 LARGE EGGPLANTS

4 CUPS FLOUR

8 EGGS (BEATEN)

16 0Z. VEGETABLE OIL

6 CUPS MARINARA SAUCE (SEE RECIPE PG. 176)

1 LB. MOZZARELLA (SLICED THIN)

¼ CUP PECORINO ROMANO CHEESE (GRATED)


WASH AND PEEL EGGPLANT, THEN SLICE INTO ¼ INCH SLICES. DREDGE IN FLOUR. SOAK IN EGG FOR 10 MINUTES. ADD OIL TO LARGE FRYING PAN ON MEDIUM HEAT. WHEN OIL IS HOT, ADD ENOUGH EGGPLANT TO FIT IN PAN WITHOUT OVERLAPPING. SAUTÉ ON EACH SIDE ABOUT 2 MINUTES, OR UNTIL EGG IS GOLDEN IN COLOR. CONTINUE PROCESS UNTIL ALL EGGPLANT IS COOKED.

IN A 12 INCH WIDE BY 3 INCH DEEP BAKING PAN, LADLE 1 CUP SAUCE TO COVER BOTTOM OF PAN. LAYER 1 ROW OF EGGPLANT, THEN A LAYER OF MOZZARELLA. TOP WITH A LAYER OF SAUCE, THEN ANOTHER LAYER OF EGGPLANT, A LAYER OF MOZZARELLA, TOP WITH ANOTHER OF SAUCE. FINALLY, ONE

MORE LAYER OF EGGPLANT, LAYER OF MOZZARELLA, AND REMAINING SAUCE. TOP WITH ¼ CUP OF ROMANO CHEESE. (3 ROWS ALL TOGETHER) BAKE IN PREHEATED OVEN AT 375 DEGREES FOR 1 HOUR.

SERVES 4 TO 6.

## THINGS OF INTEREST

Many Italian immigrants came to Philadelphia at the turn of the century as unskilled laborers—and the rapidly growing city needed them badly. Employment brokers (*Padrones*) hired them in Italy and sent them to America. Italians played a key role in building the Broad Street Subway, the Market-Frankford El, City Hall, and the Reading Terminal. They worked long, hard hours for meager wages.

# SAUSAGE AND PEPPERS

1 ½ LB. SWEET ITALIAN SAUSAGE

2 CUPS VEGETABLE OIL

2 LARGE GREEN BELL PEPPERS (SLICED)

1 SMALL SPANISH ONION (SLICED)

4 CUPS MARINARA SAUCE (SEE RECIPE PG. 176)

1 CUP WATER

CUT SAUSAGE INTO 2 INCH PIECES. PAN FRY SAUSAGE WITH OIL ON MEDIUM HEAT FOR 5 MINUTES, TURNING OCCASIONALLY TO MAKE SURE ALL SIDES GET COOKED. DRAIN OIL. ADD PEPPERS AND ONIONS, AND CONTINUE TO SAUTÉ FOR 1 MORE MINUTE, STIRRING CONSTANTLY. AT THIS POINT, ADD MARINARA SAUCE AND WATER. BRING TO A BOIL, LOWER FLAME, AND SIMMER FOR 10 MINUTES.

SERVES 2 TO 3.

# SWEETBREADS

2 LBS. CLEANED SWEETBREADS

2 QTS. WATER

¾ CUP OLIVE OIL

1 CUP WHITE FLOUR

½ CUP SAUTERNE WINE

½ LB. BUTTER

4 CLOVES GARLIC (MINCED)

1 LEVEL TEASPOON BLACK PEPPER

1 LEVEL TEASPOON SALT

1 LB. WHITE MUSHROOMS

1 LEMON (QUARTERED)

½ CUP FRESH PARSLEY

BOIL 2 LBS. OF SWEETBREADS IN 4 QT. POT FOR 30 MINUTES. WHEN FINISHED, COOL, RINSE, AND TRIM EXCESS FAT. SLICE SWEETBREADS INTO ½ INCH ME-DALLIONS, THEN SLICE MUSHROOMS. IN 18 INCH, NON-STICK FRYING PAN, ADD ¾ CUP OLIVE OIL. WHEN OIL IS HOT, LOWER FLAME TO MEDIUM. DREDGE SWEETBREADS IN FLOUR, AND ADD TO PAN. SAUTÉ ON BOTH SIDES UNTIL GOLDEN BROWN. THEN, DRAIN PAN OF OIL, AT WHICH POINT DEGLAZE PAN WITH ½ CUP SAUTERNE WINE. THEN ADD ½ LB. BUTTER, SALT, BLACK PEPPER, GARLIC, AND MUSHROOMS. SAUTÉ ALL INGREDIENTS TOGETHER FOR 2 MINUTES. SERVE GAR-NISHED WITH PARSLEY AND QUARTERED LEMONS. SERVES 4.

# TRIPE NEAPOLITAN

"... This old world favorite, if you didn't know, is the lining of the cow's stomach. If you never had it, now is the time to try it. It's delicious ..."

2 LBS. HONEYCOMB TRIPE

8 CUPS MARINARA SAUCE (SEE RECIPE PG. 176)

WASH AND SLICE TRIPE INTO ½ INCH X 3 INCH SLICES. IN LARGE SAUCE POT, ADD TRIPE AND MARINARA SAUCE. BRING TO A BOIL, LOWER FLAME, AND SIMMER FOR 45 MINUTES, OR UNTIL TENDER. (COOKING TIMES VARY)

## *WHAT THEY MEAN . . .*

**Trippa** - (TREEP-ah) The Italian word for Tripe.

# VEAL KIDNEYS WITH PEPPERS

". . . When prepping the kidneys, make sure to cut it into pieces and trim away the inner fat between them. Also, make sure they are as fresh as possible. They should have a purple tint to them . . ."

2 LBS. VEAL KIDNEYS

1 QT. WATER

2 LARGE GREEN BELL PEPPERS (SLICED)

1 LARGE SPANISH ONION (SLICED)

½ CUP VEGETABLE OIL

½ CUP SAUTERNE WINE

½ LB. BUTTER

1 TEASPOON SALT

¾ TEASPOON BLACK PEPPER

¾ TEASPOON OREGANO

IN LARGE POT, BOIL KIDNEYS FOR 6 MINUTES WITH 1 QT. WATER. WHILE KIDNEYS ARE BOILING, SAUTÉ PEPPERS AND ONION WITH OIL FOR 2 MINUTES, STIRRING CONSTANTLY. WHEN KIDNEYS ARE DONE, DRAIN AND ADD TO PAN WITH PEPPERS AND ONION. DEGLAZE PAN WITH WINE. ADD BUTTER, SALT, BLACK PEPPER, AND OREGANO, AND CONTINUE TO SAUTÉ FOR 3 MINUTES.

SERVES 4 TO 6.

Unbeaten Heavyweight Champion Rocky Marciano, seated second from left, is pictured with Ralph and a full contingent of admirers.

Dom DeLuise, center, paid Ralph's a surprise visit.

# CHAPTER 15

## Rice and Polenta

*One of the staple dishes of the ancient Romans was "Pulmentum," a kind of mush made from grain—usually millet or spelt—an early type of wheat—and, sometimes, chick pea-flour. It may not have been inspiring, but it nourished the conquerors of the ancient world. It was, in a sense, the soldier's field ration. The modern version of Pulmentum is called Polenta, and it can be eaten either soft and heated, with the consistency of mashed potatoes, or hard and cold, when it can be sliced like a cake.*

## BASIC POLENTA

8 CUPS WATER
1 TABLESPOON EXTRA VIRGIN OLIVE OIL
1 TABLESPOON SALT
1 ½ CUPS COARSE YELLOW CORN MEAL

IN MEDIUM POT, BRING 4 CUPS WATER, 1-TABLE-SPOON OLIVE OIL, AND 1 TABLESPOON SALT TO A BOIL. LOWER FLAME TO MEDIUM AND SLOWLY ADD CORN-

MEAL TO POT, STIRRING CONSTANTLY (DO NOT LET LUMPS FORM). TAKE ALL THE TIME YOU NEED TO ADD CORNMEAL. AT THIS POINT, THE MIXTURE SHOULD START TO PERK OR BUBBLE.

KEEP STIRRING AND START TO ADD WATER SLOWLY, A LITTLE AT A TIME. IT SHOULD TAKE 15 MINUTES TO COOK POLENTA. MAKE SURE TO ADD WATER SLOWLY ENOUGH TO LAST THE 15 MINUTES OF COOKING TIME. WHEN CORNMEAL IS COOKED, IT SHOULD BE SMOOTH AND FREE OF LUMPS.

SERVES 6.

**Note:** If you require more water than the recipe calls for, feel free to add it.

## THINGS OF INTEREST

At the turn of the century, it was not uncommon for Italians to come to America, earn money, and then return to their homeland. In 1904, ten per cent of the Italians entering the United States had been here before. It was not unusual for Ralph's to bring in someone to work in the kitchen, provide them with a room in their third floor hotel, and at some point see them return to Italy due to homesickness, or simply because they had earned enough money to provide for their needs.

# BAKED POLENTA

## POLENTA (SEE RECIPE PG. 167)

WHEN POLENTA IS FINISHED, POUR INTO LIGHTLY OILED BAKING PAN (12 INCHES X 10 INCHES) AND SPREAD EVENLY. PLACE IN PREHEATED OVEN AT 375 DEGREES. BAKE FOR 30 MINUTES UNTIL LIGHTLY BROWN AND CRISPY. SLICE INTO SQUARES AND SERVE AS A SIDE DISH, TOPPED WITH TOMATO SAUCE OR BUTTER.

# POLENTA WITH TOMATO SAUCE AND MEAT BALLS

POLENTA (SEE RECIPE PG. 167)
12 MEAT BALLS (SEE RECIPE PG. 114)
6 CUPS TOMATO SAUCE (SEE RECIPE PG. 179)
½ CUP PECORINO ROMANO CHEESE (GRATED)

HEAT TOMATO SAUCE AND MEAT BALLS IN POT. BRING TO A BOIL, LOWER FLAME, AND ALLOW TO SIMMER, STIRRING CONSTANTLY. WHEN POLENTA IS FINISHED, SERVE IN LARGE BOWLS. ADD 2 MEAT BALLS TO EACH BOWL AND TOP WITH SAUCE AND CHEESE.
SERVES 6.

# RISOTTO WITH PORCINI MUSHROOMS

1 CUP DRY PORCINI MUSHROOMS

1 CUP WATER

1 LARGE SPANISH ONION (CHOPPED)

¼ CUP EXTRA VIRGIN OLIVE OIL

8 FRESH BASIL LEAVES (CHOPPED)

2 ½ CUPS ARBORIO RICE

8 CUPS VEAL STOCK OR CHICKEN BROTH (SEE RECIPE)

¼ CUP HEAVY CREAM

1 TEASPOON SALT (OR AS NEEDED)

½ TEASPOON BLACK PEPPER

SOAK MUSHROOMS IN CUP OF WARM WATER FOR 20 MINUTES. WHILE MUSHROOMS ARE SOAKING, SAUTÉ ONION IN OLIVE OIL UNTIL SLIGHTLY BROWN.ADD FRESH BASIL AND SAUTE FOR 1 MINUTE. ADD RICE AND STIR UNTIL RICE IS COATED WITH THE OIL. ADD 6 CUPS OF VEAL STOCK OR CHICKEN BROTH (KEEP 2 CUPS IN RESERVE), MUSHROOMS WITH WATER, CREAM, SALT, AND BLACK PEPPER. BRING TO A BOIL, LOWER FLAME AND SIMMER, STIRRING CONSTANTLY. AS RICE BEGINS TO THICKEN, ADD A LITTLE BROTH. YOU WILL NEED TO USE ALL THE BROTH (BUT DO NOT ADD ALL AT ONCE). RICE SHOULD TAKE ABOUT 40 MINUTES TO COOK, BUT KEEP CHECKING. IT IS DONE WHEN RICE IS AL DENTE (FIRM BUT NOT HARD).

SERVES 6.

**Note:** If you use all the veal stock indicated in the ingredients, keep extra on hand and add slowly until rice is done.

# CHAPTER 16

## Sauces

*In South Philadelphia you have "gravy" with your pasta . . . not "sauce," but that's probably a local thing. In the old days, the poor people often skipped the main course of their meal and filled themselves with pasta—which served to satisfy their hunger. The pasta was usually accompanied by a sauce that afforded them the taste of what the main course might have included—bits of chopped meat, tiny clams, and so forth—had they been able to afford it.*

*Today, things are different . . . but we still love our sauces . . .*

*The following sauces are primarily used with pastas, but at Ralph's we also use them for veal, chicken, or any dish that you can think of.*

*Just use your imagination . . .*

# CAPRICCIOSA SAUCE

1 LARGE SPANISH ONION (CHOPPED)

1 CUP EXTRA VIRGIN OLIVE OIL

3-28 OZ. CANS TOMATOES (CRUSHED BY HAND)

½ CUP FRESH BASIL (CHOPPED)

IF FRESH ISN'T AVAILABLE, USE 1 TEASPOON DRY

1 ½ TABLESPOONS SALT

1 TEASPOON BLACK PEPPER

½ CUP FRESH PARSLEY (CHOPPED)

1 TEASPOON OREGANO

SAUTÉ ONION WITH 1 CUP OLIVE OIL IN 4 QT. SAUCE POT. WHEN ONION IS GOLDEN IN COLOR, ADD TOMATOES, BASIL, SALT, BLACK PEPPER, FRESH PARSLEY, AND OREGANO. BRING TO A BOIL. LOWER FLAME AND SAUTÉ FOR 1 HOUR, STIRRING CONSTANTLY.

## *WHAT THEY MEAN . . .*

**Pesto** - (PEHS-toh) Paste. A specialty of Genoa.
**Pasta Asciutta** - (PAH-stah ahs-CHOOT-TAH) is dry pasta served plain or with little sauce.

# TRADITIONAL FETTUCINE ALFREDO SAUCE

1 QT. CREAM (HEAVY)

¼ POUND BUTTER

¾ CUP ROMANO CHEESE

1 TABLESPOON WHITE PEPPER

2 TABLESPOONS OF CORNSTARCH

½ CUP WATER (COLD)

¼ CUP PARSLEY (FRESH)

BRING A QUART OF HEAVY CREAM AND ¼ POUND OF BUTTER TO A BOIL IN SAUCEPOT. ONCE BOILING, LOWER HEAT TO A SIMMER. ADD ROMANO CHEESE AND WHITE PEPPER. MIX CORNSTARCH WITH ¼ CUP OF COLD WATER, STIRRING UNTIL SMOOTH, AND ADD TO POT. WHISK UNTIL IT COMES BACK TO A BOIL AND THICKENS. MIX WITH 3 POUNDS FETTUCINE (EGG, NOT DRY SEMOLINA). TOP WITH MORE ROMANO AND PARSLEY.

SERVES 4 TO 6.

## OTHER ALFREDO IDEAS

SAUTÉ 8 BACON STRIPS IN FRYING PAN, THEN PU-REE WITH A SMALL HANDFUL OF FRESH BASIL LEAVES AND ½ CUP OF WATER. ADD TO ABOVE RECIPE.

OR . . .

TAKE THE TRADITIONAL RECIPE, ADD A CUP OF ROASTED RED PEPPERS (DRAINED OF OIL) AND 6 AR-TICHOKE HEARTS, QUARTERED. INSTEAD OF SERVING WITH FETTUCINE, SERVE ON CHICKEN BREAST OR VEAL.

## *DID YOU KNOW???*

It is hard to imagine modern Italian cooking without the tomato, yet no European had ever set eyes on one until Spanish Conquista-dor Cortez conquered Mexico in 1554 and returned home with them. The first Italian description of a tomato was *pomo d'oro* (golden apple) and the first tomato in Europe was golden in color and about the size of a cherry. It took the Italians close to two centuries to develop a new, bigger, red variety and to use it in cooking. Not surprisingly, the first use for it was in salads.

# MARINARA SAUCE

1 LARGE SPANISH ONION (CHOPPED)
6 TO 8 LARGE GARLIC CLOVES (MINCED)
VIRGIN OLIVE OIL
3-28 OZ. CANS TOMATOES (CRUSHED BY HAND)
½ CUP FRESH BASIL (CHOPPED)
IF FRESH ISN'T AVAILABLE, USE 1 TEASPOON OF DRY BASIL
1 TEASPOON SALT
1 TEASPOON PEPPER
1 TEASPOON OREGANO
½ CUP FRESH PARSLEY (CHOPPED)
3 TABLESPOONS TOMATO PASTE

SAUTÉ ONIONS AND GARLIC WITH 1 CUP OLIVE OIL IN 4 QT. SAUCE POT. WHEN ONIONS AND GARLIC ARE GOLDEN IN COLOR, ADD TOMATOES, BASIL, SALT, BLACK PEPPER, OREGANO, FRESH PARSLEY, AND TOMATO PASTE. BRING TO A BOIL, LOWER FLAME AND SIMMER FOR 1 HOUR, STIRRING CONSTANTLY.

# PESTO SAUCE

16 OZ. VEGETABLE OIL
1 LARGE BUNCH FRESH BASIL
½ CUP PINOLE (PINE) NUTS
1 TABLESPOON SALT
1 TEASPOON BLACK PEPPER
1 TEASPOON OREGANO
8 CLOVES GARLIC (MINCED)

IN BLENDER OR FOOD PROCESSOR, PUREE 8 OZ.
OIL, FRESH BASIL, PINE NUTS, SALT, BLACK PEPPER, AND
OREGANO. IN LARGE FRYING PAN, SAUTÉ 8 OZ. OIL AND
GARLIC CLOVES UNTIL GARLIC IS GOLDEN IN COLOR.
ADD PUREED BASIL AND PINE NUT MIXTURE AND
BRING BACK TO A BOIL. SAUTÉ FOR 3 MINUTES. SERVE
ON YOUR FAVORITE PASTA.
    SERVES 4 TO 6.

## *THINGS OF INTEREST*

Saturday night dances at Bishop Nuemann High School regularly
drew a thousand or more teenagers during the 1950's and 60's.
Native sons, such as Frankie Avalon and Fabian, were among the
weekly guest artists provided by record promoters seeking to spike
sales of their 45's. Another native son, Jerry "The Geator with the
Heator" Blavat, got his start doing record hops at St. Elizabeth's
Church and then went on to greater glory at the Chez Vous Ball-
room as well as fame on the radio and TV.

# POMODORO SAUCE (BLUSH)

4 LARGE TOMATOES (SLICED)

12 FRESH BASIL LEAVES (CHOPPED)

½ LB. BUTTER

½ CUP SAUTERNE WINE

4 CUPS HEAVY CREAM

¾ TABLESPOON SALT

1 TEASPOON BLACK PEPPER

1 TEASPOON OREGANO

4 TABLESPOONS COOKED GARLIC (SEE RECIPE PG 93)

¼ CUP FRESH PARSLEY (CHOPPED)

IN MEDIUM POT, SAUTÉ TOMATOES AND BASIL WITH BUTTER FOR 3 MINUTES ON MEDIUM FLAME. AT THIS POINT, DEGLAZE PAN WITH SAUTERNE WINE, ADD REMAINING INGREDIENTS, AND SIMMER ON LOW FLAME FOR 5 MINUTES, STIRRING CONSTANTLY.CAN BE SERVED ON CHICKEN, VEAL OR PASTA.SERVES 4.

# TOMATO SAUCE WITH MEAT

1 LARGE SPANISH ONION (CHOPPED)

6 TO 8 LARGE GARLIC CLOVES (MINCED)

1 CUP EXTRA VIRGIN OLIVE OIL

1 LB. GROUND VEAL, BEEF, AND PORK (MIXED)

3-28 OZ. CANS TOMATOES (CRUSHED BY HAND)

1 BUNCH FRESH BASIL (CHOPPED)

IF FRESH NOT AVAILABLE, USE 1 TEASPOON DRY BASIL

1 ½ TABLESPOONS SALT

1 TEASPOON BLACK PEPPER

1 TEASPOON CRUSHED FENNEL SEED

½ CUP FRESH PARSLEY (CHOPPED)

3 TABLESPOONS TOMATO PASTE

SAUTÉ ONION AND GARLIC CLOVES WITH 1 CUP OF OLIVE OIL IN 4 QT. SAUCE POT, FOR 3 MINUTES. ADD GROUND MEAT AND SAUTÉ UNTIL MEAT IS BROWNED, STIRRING CONSTANTLY. ADD TOMATOES, BASIL, SALT, BLACK PEPPER, CRUSHED FENNEL, FRESH PARSLEY, AND TOMATO PASTE. BRING TO A BOIL, LOWER FLAME, AND SIMMER FOR 1 HOUR, STIRRING CONSTANTLY.

# CHAPTER 17

## *Omelets*

*The ancient Romans loved all sorts of condiments and spices—still do to this day -but they had no cane or beet sugar. Instead, they had to make do with grape syrup (defrutum) and honey, which they ate with great enthusiasm and zeal throughout their meals. They also invented deserts that remain in use to this day, one of which added an important word to cooking—Omelet— which comes from "ova mellita" which means, literally, "honeyed eggs."*

## GIAMBOTTE (EGG OMELET)

12 EGGS

2 CUPS VEGETABLE OIL

2 CHICKEN BREASTS

1 LB. SAUSAGE

2 LARGE RED BELL PEPPERS (SLICED)

8 WHITE MUSHROOMS (SLICED)

1 LARGE SPANISH ONION (SLICED)

8 JUMBO SHRIMP (PEELED, CLEANED, AND DEVEINED)

¼ CUP PECORINO ROMANO CHEESE (GRATED)

2 TABLESPOONS COOKED GARLIC (SEE RECIPE)
½ TEASPOON BLACK PEPPER
¼ CUP FRESH PARSLEY (CHOPPED)
¼ CUP FRESH BASIL (CHOPPED)

IN 2 SEPARATE FRYING PANS, SAUTÉ CHICKEN AND
SAUSAGE WITH 1 CUP VEGETABLE OIL EACH. WHEN
CHICKEN AND SAUSAGE ARE DONE, PLACE ON PAPER
TOWELS TO DRAIN OIL. BEAT EGGS IN LARGE MIXING
BOWL WITH CHEESE, GARLIC, BLACK PEPPER, PARSLEY,
BASIL, PEPPERS, MUSHROOMS, AND ONIONS. SPRAY
BOTTOM OF 18 INCH FRYING PAN WITH NON-STICK
SPRAY AND POUR EGG MIXTURE INTO PAN. PLACE
CHICKEN, SAUSAGE, AND RAW SHRIMP IN A DECORA-
TIVE PATTERN IN EGG MIXTURE. BAKE IN PREHEATED
OVEN AT 375 DEGREES FOR 40 MINUTES.
SERVES 4 TO 6.

## THINGS OF INTEREST

The pimento, or red pepper, so important in Italian cooking, was
also one of the finds of the Spanish Conquistadors. The potato was
also sent back to Europe from the New World in 1540. Originally
described as a "small truffle," the Germans still call potatoes and
truffles by the same name, *kartoffel*. In Italy, potatoes were known
as *tartufoli* but today are known as *patata* (pah-TAH-tah).

# PEPPERS AND EGGS

"... This dish can be eaten as a sandwich or like we used to do, as a dinner by itself with Italian bread on the side ..."

2 LARGE GREEN BELL PEPPERS (SLICED)

¼ CUP VEGETABLE OIL

12 EGGS

2 TABLESPOONS PECORINO ROMANO CHEESE (GRATED)

1 TABLESPOON COOKED GARLIC (SEE RECIPE PG. 93)

1 TEASPOON BLACK PEPPER

1 TEASPOON OREGANO


SAUTÉ PEPPERS WITH OIL IN LARGE FRYING PAN FOR 3 MINUTES. WHILE PEPPERS ARE COOKING, BEAT EGGS, CHEESE, GARLIC, BLACK PEPPER, AND OREGANO. ADD EGGS TO PAN WITH PEPPERS. LOWER FLAME, COVER PAN WITH LID, AND COOK UNTIL EGGS ARE NO LONGER WET INSIDE.

SERVES 4 TO 6.

# CHAPTER 18

## *Deserts*

*It was from the Arabs, as early as the Ninth century, that the Southern Italians learned how to concoct the deserts which became such a vital and important part of their cuisine. The art of making ice cream, for example, was learned from the Arabs, who had learned it from the Chinese. They also introduced various sweets based on honey and brought sugar cane as a crop to Europe. As time went by, the Italians saved elaborate desserts for honored guests or special occasions and they finished their meals with either cheese or fruit.*

## BISCOTTI

½ LB. BUTTER

4 EGGS

3 ½ CUPS FLOUR

1 TABLESPOON BAKING POWDER

1 TABLESPOON LEMON JUICE

¼ CUP VANILLA

MELT BUTTER ON LOW HEAT (DO NOT ALLOW TO GET HOT). POUR INTO MIXING BOWL AND WHISK IN EGGS, LEMON JUICE, AND VANILLA. AT THIS POINT, BEGIN TO ADD FLOUR SLOWLY. WHEN DOUGH STARTS TO FORM, KNEAD WITH HANDS UNTIL ALL INGREDIENTS ARE MIXED WELL AND DOUGH IS FORMED. REFRIGERATE FOR 2 HOURS. DIVIDE DOUGH INTO 4 LOAVES, ½ INCH HIGH BY 2 INCHES WIDE. GREASE BOTTOM OF BAKING PAN AND BAKE IN PREHEATED OVEN AT 350 DEGREES FOR 30 MINUTES. LET COOL. CUT DIAGONAL, ¾ INCH THICK, SLICES AND ARRANGE ON THEIR SIDE. BAKE ON EACH SIDE FOR 4 MINUTES.

## THINGS OF INTEREST

St. Mary Magdalen de Pazzi was the official name of the first church in South Philadelphia, established because of the nationality of its parishioners. Known as St. Mary's, it was founded in 1852 and named after a 15th Century Florentine Saint. The church was located on Marriott Street, between 7th and 8th streets (today known as Montrose Street, the same street where Francesco Dispigno first opened his restaurant). It was the first Italian Catholic Church in the nation. Bishop John Neumann appointed The Reverend Gaetano Mariani as first pastor.

# EASTER BREAD

1 CUP WARM WATER

2 PACKAGES YEAST

6 CUPS ALL PURPOSE FLOUR

¾ CUP SHORTENING

1 CUP GRANULATED SUGAR

1 TEASPOON SALT

2 EGGS

1 EGG WHITE

1 EGG YOLK

2 TABLESPOONS ANISE SEED

COMBINE YEAST WITH ½ CUP WATER. LET STAND FOR 5 TO 10 MINUTES. IN LARGE MIXING BOWL, ADD ½ CUP WATER AND 1 ½ CUPS FLOUR. ADD THE YEAST TO THIS MIXTURE. COVER BOWL WITH A TOWEL AND PLACE IN A WARM PLACE FOR 2 HOURS. COMBINE THE SUGAR, SALT, AND SHORTENING, BEAT WELL AND ADD 2 EGGS AND 1 EGG WHITE. AT THIS POINT, ADD 4 ½ CUPS FLOUR AND ANISE SEED TO SHORTENING MIXTURE AND COMBINE WITH YEAST MIXTURE. KNEAD DOUGH UNTIL ALL INGREDIENTS ARE BLENDED AND DOUGH IS SOFT. LET THE DOUGH RAISE OVERNIGHT.

IN THE MORNING, SEPARATE DOUGH INTO 2 PIECES. ROLL INTO 2 ROPES, EACH ½ INCH THICK, AND MAKE INTO A BRAID. TOP THE BRAID WITH THE EGG YOLK USING A PASTRY BRUSH, AND BAKE IN PRE-HEATED OVEN AT 350 DEGREES FOR 30 MINUTES.

# ITALIAN CREAM CAKE

## SPONGE CAKE

12 EGGS

2 CUPS SUGAR

2 CUPS FLOUR

2 TEASPOONS BAKING POWDER

2 TEASPOONS VANILLA

1 CUP LIGHT RUM

## VANILLA CREAM

1 PINT MILK

½ CUP FLOUR

½ CUP SUGAR

2 EGG YOLKS

1 TEASPOON VANILLA

## CHOCOLATE CREAM

1 QT MILK

1 CUP FLOUR

1 ½ CUPS SUGAR

3 EGG YOLKS

3 SQUARES BAKING CHOCOLATE

## SPONGE CAKE

SEPARATE THE EGGS. PUT THE EGG YOLKS IN MEDIUM MIXING BOWL AND BEAT UNTIL THICK. ADD

SUGAR. BEAT THE EGG WHITES IN LARGE MIXING BOWL UNTIL STIFF. FOLD HALF THE EGG WHITES INTO THE EGG YOLKS UNTIL MIXED. SIFT THE FLOUR. FOLD INTO THE YOLK MIXTURE WITH THE BAKING POWDER. AFTER IT IS ALL MIXED, FOLD IN REMAINING EGG WHITES. POUR INTO GREASED BAKING PAN AND BAKE IN PREHEATED OVEN AT 350 DEGREES FOR 35 MINUTES.

## VANILLA CREAM

BEAT THE EGG YOLKS. ADD MILK, FLOUR, SUGAR, AND VANILLA. MIX WELL. STIR OVER MEDIUM HEAT UNTIL THICK.

## CHOCOLATE CREAM

BEAT THE EGG YOLKS. ADD MILK, FLOUR, SUGAR, AND CHOCOLATE SQUARES. MIX WELL. STIR OVER MEDIUM HEAT UNTIL CHOCOLATE IS MELTED AND BECOMES THICK.

## TO ASSEMBLE CAKE

CUT CAKE INTO 3 LAYERS. SPRINKLE EACH LAYER WITH RUM. SPREAD BOTTOM ROW WITH CHOCOLATE CREAM, PLACE LAYER OF SPONGE CAKE ON TOP. SPREAD NEXT LAYER WITH VANILLA CREAM. PLACE LAST SPONGE LAYER ON TOP AND FINISH WHOLE CAKE, INCLUDING SIDES, WITH REMAINING CHOCOLATE CREAM.

## PEACHSICLE

1-16 OZ. CAN PEACHES IN SYRUP
¼ CUP PEACH SCHNAPPS
1 CUP HEAVY CREAM
4 CUPS VANILLA ICE CREAM

ADD PEACHES WITH SYRUP AND PEACH SCHNAPPS TO A BLENDER. PUREE MIXTURE UNTIL LIQUEFIED. POUR INTO SMALL POT AND ADD CREAM. BRING TO A BOIL. LET COOL AND REFRIGERATE OVER NIGHT. SERVE ON VANILLA ICE CREAM.

## THINGS OF INTEREST

In 1994, Palumbo's, the city's oldest nightclub—and a South Philadelphia landmark—was destroyed by fire. For many years, Ralph's would stay open until 4:30am to accommodate the entertainers and the staff from the club whose day was just ending at that time. It was not unusual to see a steady stream of people heading for Ralph's when the CR Club closed.

# AUNT ELLIE'S PIZZELLES

". . . Having Pizzelle around the house meant only one thing—Christmas must be right around the corner. Every year, like clockwork, the day after Thanksgiving, Aunt Ellie would begin her ritual of making Pizzelles. When I eat these today they still bring back great memories of growing up. First it was my Grandmother Mary and then my Aunt Ellie took over the ritual . . ."

6 EGGS (BEATEN)

1 ½ CUPS SUGAR

1 CUP VEGETABLE OIL

2 TABLESPOONS VANILLA EXTRACT

2 TABLESPOONS ANISE SEEDS

4 TEASPOONS BAKING POWDER

3 ½ CUPS FLOUR

(PREHEAT PIZZELLE IRON FOR AT LEAST 15 MINUTES BEFORE STARTING) AFTER BEATING 6 EGGS, ADD SUGAR, OIL, VANILLA EXTRACT, ANISE SEEDS, AND BAKING POWDER. BEAT INGREDIENTS TOGETHER AND WHILE BEATING, ADD FLOUR. BEAT UNTIL ALL INGREDIENTS ARE MIXED AND A LOOSE DOUGH HAS FORMED. ADD A HEAPING TEASPOON OF DOUGH TO PIZZELLE IRON AND COOK UNTIL A LIGHT GOLDEN BROWN. WHEN DONE, CAREFULLY PICK OFF IRON WITH A FORK, AND LAY ON FLAT SURFACE TO COOL. REPEAT THIS PROCESS UNTIL ALL DOUGH IS GONE. (NOTE: THE AMOUNT OF DOUGH YOU USE IS DETER-

MINED BY WHETHER A WHOLE PIZZELLE IS FORMED. IF NOT, MORE DOUGH NEEDS TO BE ADDED. IF THE DOUGH COMES OUT THE SIDES OF THE IRON, LESS DOUGH IS NEEDED. WILL MAKE ABOUT 60 TO 70 PIZZELLES.

## THINGS OF INTEREST

Our Lady of Good Counsel Roman Catholic Church was opened in 1898 and was located between St. Mary's and St. Paul's (which had been founded in 1847), on the 800 block of Christian Street. The building was actually a school, which was purchased from St. Paul's. The church closed in 1933, but for 35 years was reputed to be the busiest Catholic Church in Philadelphia.

# RICOTTA CANNOLI

(NOTE: TO SIMPLIFY THIS RECIPE, STORE BOUGHT
    CANNOLI SHELLS WILL BE USED)
2 LBS. RICOTTA CHEESE
1 CUP SUGAR
3 TEASPOONS VANILLA
¼ CUP MINIATURE CHOCOLATE PIECES
CONFECTIONERS SUGAR

COMBINE AND BEAT TOGETHER THE RICOTTA,
SUGAR, AND VANILLA. STIR IN THE CHOCOLATE PIECES.
REFRIGERATE FOR 2 HOURS. JUST BEFORE SERVING,
FILL CANNOLI SHELLS WITH RICOTTA FILLING, MAK-
ING SURE TO FILL ALL THE WAY TO THE MIDDLE.
SPRINKLE WITH CONFECTIONERS SUGAR. MAKES
ABOUT 10 CANNOLIS.

# RICOTTA PIE

3 LBS. RICOTTA

½ CUP FLOUR

2 TABLEPOON VANILLA EXTRACT

1 TEASPOON LEMON EXTRACT

1 PINT LIGHT CREAM

2 CUPS SUGAR

9 EGGS

BEAT THE EGGS UNTIL THICK. ADD SUGAR AND BEAT WELL. ADD VANILLA AND LEMON EXTRACTS, CREAM, FLOUR, AND RICOTTA. MIX WELL. POUR MIXTURE INTO GREASED BAKING PAN AND BAKE IN PREHEATED OVEN AT 350 DEGREES FOR 1 ½ HOURS.

# TIRA MISU

24 ITALIAN LADYFINGERS

1 ½ CUPS ESPRESSO (COOLED)

6 EGGS (SEPARATED)

1 LB. MASCARPONE CHEESE

3 TABLESPOONS SUGAR

2 TABLESPOONS KAHLÚA

2 TABLESPOONS TIRA MISU LIQUEUR

2 TABLESPOONS BRANDY

1 TEASPOON ORANGE EXTRACT

8 OZ. BITTERSWEET CHOCOLATE (CHOPPED)


DIP 12 LADYFINGERS IN ESPRESSO. ARRANGE ON A FLAT SERVING PLATTER IN A ROW. MIX EGG YOLKS WITH SUGAR UNTIL PALE IN COLOR. ADD MASCARPONE CHEESE, ALL 3 LIQUEURS, AND ORANGE EXTRACT. MIX THOROUGHLY.

BEAT EGG WHITES UNTIL STIFF, BUT NOT DRY. FOLD WHITES INTO MASCARPONE MIXTURE. SPREAD HALF THE MASCARPONE MIXTURE ON TOP LADYFIN-GERS. SPRINKLE HALF THE CHOCOLATE ON TOP. DIP THE REMAINING LADYFINGERS INTO ESPRESSO. RE-PEAT LAYERING WITH LADYFINGERS AND MASCARPONE CHEESE, AND TOP WITH REMAINING CHOCOLATE.

COVER WITH FOIL AND REFRIGERATE OVERNIGHT. SERVES 10 TO 12

# ZABAGLIONE

10 EGG YOLKS

¾ CUP SUPER FINE SUGAR

1 CUP MARSALA WINE

½ TEASPOON VANILLA EXTRACT

½ LEMON PEEL (GRATED)

CINNAMON (PINCH)

1 CUP HEAVY CREAM (WHIPPED).

PLACE THE FIRST 3 INGREDIENTS IN THE TOP OF A DOUBLE BOILER—IT SHOULD BE A ROUND-BOT-TOMED METAL BOWL THAT WILL FIT THE POT. PLACE OVER HOT, NOT BOILING, WATER. THE BOTTOM OF BOWL SHOULD NOT TOUCH WATER. BEAT WITH A WIRE WHISK, SCRAPING THE SIDES AND BOTTOM CON-STANTLY, UNTIL IT REACHES THE POINT WHERE IT FORMS SOFT PEAKS LIKE A MERINGUE.

REMOVE FROM STOVE AND CONTINUE TO BEAT UNTIL COOL. AT THIS POINT, ADD VANILLA, LEMON PEEL, AND CINNAMON.

PLACE MIXING BOWL INTO LARGER BOWL WITH CRACKED ICE, AND CONTINUE BEATING UNTIL MIX-TURE IS CHILLED THROUGH.

BEAT THE HEAVY CREAM UNTIL STILL, AND FOLD INTO THE ZABAIONE. CHILL FOR 2 HOURS OR UNTIL READY TO SERVE. MAY BE SERVED ON STRAWBERRIES OR BLUEBERRIES.

# CHAPTER 19

## *"What Our Friends Say About us . . ."*

In July, 1999, Ralph's website was created (**www.ralphsrestaurant.com**) and it has provided a forum for our friends—old and new—to tell us what they like about Ralph's. While we have had well over one hundred individual messages, we have taken some of the most representative and reprinted them here so that you can get a sense of what the "Ralph's Tradition" is all about.

\*     \*     \*

**John DiSante** from Los Angeles, CA said, "I have family in Philadelphia and my Dad grew up in South Philly. Every time we go back to visit we make Ralph's our first stop. The food makes you think of home and family dinner and the service is great. There is a reason why you are the oldest Italian restaurant! You are the best . . . Thanks for some great food and great memories."

**Cheryl Gratt** from Tallahassee, FL said, "My husband's family is 200% Italian (Grattafiori) and we love the old Italian cooking! Heard about you from a friend who just visited you!"

**Pat DiGiuseppe** from Beaufort, North Carolina said, "My wife and I had dinner at Ralph's for the first time about seven years ago when our good friends, **Walt and Betty Kropp**, brought us to your restaurant. I grew up in New Jersey, am a Villanova alumnus, and travel throughout North America in my work. In our dining experience, you are the best Italian Restaurant both in food quality and service. We had dinner with you this past Saturday when we visited the Kropps. It was excellent and we enjoyed seeing Ronnie Trombino and Jimmy Rubino again."

**Bill** from "straight out of Philadelphia" said, "If you want to have the best food on the east coast, and possibly the US, come to Ralph's because it is the real deal. Believe me, I travel the US and go to all the famous restaurants in every city I'm in, and this is, without a doubt, my favorite." (Thanks Bill, even if you were too shy to give us your last name.)

**Peter Lisker** from New York City wrote, "My friend and I stumbled upon your wonderful restaurant about three weeks ago. Fortunately for us, the other two restaurants we stopped by before trying yours were both closed on Sunday and a nice man from the coffee shop across the street recommended you. When I first peeked inside, my first thought was we can't afford this—but happily I was wrong. The food and the service were excellent and so were the martinis! I also wanted to say a special thanks to our waiter, Barry, as well as the rest of the staff. The only thing shocking about the meal was that it was both delicious and so affordable. I will make it a point to stop by on my next visit to Philly. Thanks again and all the best."

**Dr. Arnold Baskies** from Cherry Hill, NJ, logged on and said, "We had a delicious dinner last night. Barry, our waiter, is one of the best at his profession. And Ronnie is the best maitre d' we have ever had, as well as being a fine human being. Your staff is excellent and is reflective of the fine ownership."

**Mikey Chang** from South Philly writes, "Ralph's Italian Restaurant is the greatest place in the world. I work at Ralph's and man it is like heaven. The managers are great and never holler at the busboys, for anything. The waiters help out the busboys, like pouring water and clearing their own tables when we are busy. It is truly a great establishment."

**Diane McElhone Shelton** from Naples, Florida, dropped by to say, "I am an old friend from Philadelphia, dating back many years. I continue to visit Ralph's whenever I am in the city. It is like being home."

**Marie Lovato** from Ontario, Canada, stopped by to say "Ciao . . . I must say I really enjoyed your site . . . 'può il vostro commercio essere benedetto con il throough di felicità e di successo esso tutto . . . avere un giorno meraviglioso, arrivederci'."

**Larraine Formica**, originally from Philadelphia, now living in Maryland, says, "We had the pleasure to eat at Ralph's twice now and it is wonderful. It's like having your (Italian) grandmother cook for you! Our son is a student at LaSalle University in the city and when he wants to take a girl to a really nice place, he chooses Ralph's."

**Michael Zungolo**, of Philadelphia, wrote, "Happy anniversary, may there be a hundred more and a hundred more after that. I can't count the number of times I've been to Ralph's, and the experience has never been anything but spectacular. The white mussels are the best I've had anywhere. My wife and I were last there with a large party in January, and the special chicken in sweet marsala sauce with spinach and tomatoes was simply exquisite. You just keep getting better."

**Jim Davis** from Langhorne, Pa., said, "I have been dining at Ralph's off and on for the better part of 20 years, and I have never been disappointed by the experience. Last Sunday, we celebrated my wife's birthday at Ralph's and everyone enjoyed a superb meal. Your mussels in marinara and the veal rolatini got rave reviews from several members of our party—I know they are my favorites. I look forward to my next visit."

**Lawrence James Madara** from Darby, Pa., writes "My wife who is Irish cooks Italian and loves the Italian Market heard of your restaurant through the grape vine got a copy of your news letter and said save the Web Site so here I am and we'll be down to eat. So have plenty of food ready because we love to eat and drink some good wine."

**Beverly Carson**, a Philadelphia native who moved to Charleston, SC, ten years ago wrote, "Although the South is nice, I still sorely miss Ralph's and the Italian Market. Nowhere can you find good 'gravy' or Italian Bread. Hope to return home for a visit soon and enjoy all the good food I miss."

**Greg Gustave** from Scranton, Pa., didn't beat around the bush, he simply wrote, "Outstanding food and service."

On the website is information about Jimmy Rubino's cork-screw collection. **Dominic Byrne** read about it in England and e-mailed us, "Just thought I'd check up and see how you are making all that money to build up such a good corkscrew collection. Good luck with your hunting and best wishes for a very prosperous New Year. Rest assured if I ever happen to find myself in Philly I'll pop in and see if I can relieve you of some of your collection!"

Longtime Philadelphians, **Ed and Faith Wickland,** now trans-planted to Grand Haven, Michigan, came on the site to say, "We ate at your Restaurant many times when we lived in Philly and look forward to our return trips to do so again."

**Dr. Hank English** from Bass River, Mass., is a Ralph's fan and he wrote, "I travel frequently and have heard great things about your restaurant from my friends **Bob and Jinx Larive** at Fior D'Italia in San Francisco's North Beach area. The owner there told me that while they may be the oldest Italian Restaurant in America (founded in 1886), their extensive research showed that Ralph's is the oldest family owned Italian Restaurant—and the second oldest Italian restaurant—in America!! He told me I simply had to visit your restaurant. I stopped by with friends over the Christmas (1999) holidays and had the Lobster Fra Diavolo—it was the best ever! And New Englanders know a little something about lobster. Mrs. "Doctor Hank" (Maria) is Italian and she says your food is better than her Grandmother used to make- and that's saying something. Here's to another 100—and then some! Thanks to Eddie (Rubino), our waiter, for a great job. He's the best!"

**Frank Zuccarini,** a Philadelphian, is the kind of Ralph's regu-lar who keeps the torch burning. Last December (1999) he wrote, "I was Christmas shopping and stopped for lunch today. The meal was wonderful as usual. The minestrone soup and the chicken Trombino are my favorite. I will be down to see you again soon with the whole crowd. I want to wish you all a Merry Christmas, Happy New Year and congratulations on your 100 years. You guys are the BEST!!!!!"

**Jimmy Rubino** has often been told that his waitstaff should be featured on a calendar. **Gena Arnold** and her daughter **Terri** from Reading, Pa., endorse that notion, "My daughter and I often come to your restaurant. We love the delicious food (and my daughter Terri likes the busboy)."

Philadelphian **Jeff Silver** got right to the point, "We love Ralph's! It is the first place we think of, when we have an occasion to celebrate. Keep up the good work!"

Another transplanted Philadelphian, **F. S. Nophut** of Lawrenceville, GA., says, "It's been a little over one year since I moved from Queen Village down South to Georgia. Recently, I made my way back home (I'm from Philly originally) for Thanksgiving, and made it a point to dine at your establishment that following Saturday. More than walking on South Street, the dinner experience made me quite homesick. Savoring everything, I ordered my two favorites . . . the clams casino and chicken sorrento. As always, everything was beyond perfect. Thanks for the great food, the great service, and the unique ambiance that makes Ralph's such an enjoyable experience. PS- Can you find it in your heart to send me the clams casino and the chicken sorrento recipes so I may make them down here?" (Editor's note: It was requests like this that lead to the book you are reading.)

**Nancy Palumbo** from Packer Park in South Philly, right near the restaurant, wrote, "Your restaurant is by far the best known in and around South Philadelphia, and offers authentic Italian cuisine. It is always a pleasure to dine at your establishment. Here's to another hundred years."

**Amy and John McCole** are also South Philadelphians (2nd & Christian) and they added to Ms. Palumbo's sentiments, "We've been going to Ralph's for years. Our favorite memory about the restaurant is when we struggled up to Ralph's during a blizzard.

We had to strip off three layers of clothes before getting seated. Then we rolled home fat and happy."

**Lenny and Kelly Graham** from Blue Bell, PA, wrote, "I am proud to say that I have been a "regular" at Ralph's for over 20 years and have never once been disappointed with their amazing cuisine and impeccable service. Jimmy and Eddie along with their professional staff have a unique way of making you feel like family every visit. Whether it's you first or your fiftieth visit, Ralphs' is always something very special. Without a doubt, Philadelphia's finest Italian restaurant."

**Lisa** from Bucks County came to the web to say that, "My husband, Tom, and I had a wonderful night out at Ralph's. I must recommend the Shrimp Marinara. It was delicious. Our waiter, Paul was the best. Thanks Ralph's and Paul for a wonderful evening. Will come again soon."

"We were in Pennsauken NJ for a skating competition," writes **Dave** from Utica, NY, "Met my cousins at your restaurant at their suggestion. Had the best meal in many a fortnight. My wife said the Veal Marsala was the best she has ever tasted. Thanks for a great meal and a very pleasant reunion with family."

**Gina Wiseman** from Tehachapi, CA, found the Ralph's site on Yahoo and said, "I was in Italy last year and bought a cookbook "La Cucina Veneziana," and I needed a recipe for traditional alfredo sauce. I found it in my cookbook and to be sure I translated it properly, I found you recipe and I did a good job with my translation! Your site was the only one I found with the correct recipe. Thanks for being there."

**Joe McTague** a resident of Newport Beach, Ca., and a former Philadelphian, dropped in to say, "The most unbelievable Italian food- ever!!! Just got back from five days in Philly- ate at Ralph's twice. Hats off to Eddie (who graciously served me) and Jimmy who made the taste buds pop- and I mean pop. Outstanding veal, great wine. Bravo! I'll be checking the site out for recipes and plan on bringing many a client to your doors when I'm back in Philly.

"Loved your website," wrote **Daniel Soule** of Wichita, KS, "I stumbled upon it while looking for a good marinara sauce. I use one on a regular basis but wanted to try something different (rich and thick and red). Thanks for your site . . . it's great. Good Luck to you. If I ever come to Philly . . . You can bet I will visit your restaurant. Lover of Italian foods . . ." (Editor's note: Daniel's recipe is both on the website and in this book)

Australia checked in via **Tobia Trentin** who wrote, "Ciao come state vi sto scrivendo dall'Australia. Riscrivete."

**Kathy**, who isn't from Australia, but Paducah, KY, (though originally from West Chester, PA) wrote, "I was looking for some good old fashioned recipes to cook for the southerners and found some on your site." (Editor's note: and 100 more of them in this book.)

**Laura J. Wolbach** from Folsom, PA, got right to the point, "Ralph's Italian Restaurant is the best in Italian cuisine thus far."

From Cambridge, Ontario, Canada, **Kathy** writes, " I was looking for a recipe for eggplant parmigiana. I see you have it on your wonderful menu. If I ever come to Philadelphia I will make sure I come to your restaurant. Looks wonderful."

"I was born and raised on dinner at Ralph's. I love the food!" wrote **Kimberly Lattanzio** of South Philadelphia. And ex-South Philly resident **Joanne Fortunato,** from Lansdale, PA, adds "I am originally from South Philadelphia and I loved diving at Ralph's. I stop there whenever I visit my Mom."

Countless special family events have been held at Ralph's over the past 100 years and **Thomas and Francine West** of Philadelphia were among those who enjoyed the ambiance of the restaurant. Francine wrote, "I had my wedding party there and everyone LOVED their food. The Flounder Francaise was excellent."

"Jimmy and the entire staff at the restaurant are a one of a kind gem," wrote **Ryan Friedman** of Wheaton, IL, "The food is impeccable and is worth a trip from any destination. The Wine, the Pasta, and the atmosphere are the best of any restaurant I have ever eaten at!"

**Comments:** The **Ungerer family** from Bucks County, Pa., wrote, "Jimmy and Eddie are great guys and Ralph's is a great restaurant. Ronnie will make sure you get a good table and excellent service. It is THE best Italian food."

A real fan, **Tony Stango** of Yardley, Pa., wrote, "For a great night at Ralph's, ask to start your meal with an Everything Salad. Then have a bowl of mussels in Red Sauce, the Veal Rollatine, and a bottle or two or three of Opus One 1995. Hey! I'm getting hungry just thinking about it!! Maybe I'll see you there."

**Merle Richman** from Collingswood, NJ, wrote, "We have enjoyed the meals at Ralphs for many years. My family is from Philly and most of my children are still in the Delaware Valley. I grew up in Upper Darby with many Italian friends who spoke highly of Ralphs."

From Eugene, Oregon, **Nance Snell** wrote, "I love your website . . . my mouth was watering as I read the menu. I am originally from San Francisco, the grandaughter of a Sicilian immigrant."

"I just finished reading the website comments by all the visitors to your restaurant. However, my mouth is watering, as a result of all their praise of your food and service, and I look forward to visiting you. Again. Congratulations on your 100th anniversary! WOW! 100 years. Did you know that Ralph's is only 32 1/2 years younger than Canada! Bet no one ever told you THAT before! But it is true." **Meta Packer, Toronto**

Philadelphia natives **Nick & Maria**, who have relocated to Tampa, FL, wrote, "We think of Ralph's (and your awesome food) often! We just can't get that good Italian food here in Tampa! We miss our family and friends from Bucks County, but we miss the "FOOD" the most!! And you can rest assured when we are up north for a visit . . . we'll stop by! P.S. Keep your eye on that sign, you never know when it may take a trip south!!!"

**Frank and Eve Quattrone,** Editor of "Ticket" (entertainment weekly) from Willow Grove, Pa., wrote, "Dear Jimmy,-Eve and I, and certainly my dear mother, want to thank you for a most excellent evening. We thought the dinners were superb, and we were especially charmed by your company. My mother loved the whole experience. That means a lot to me. You are a very special young man, Jimmy. Thank you for taking us into your family—even for one grand evening. I only hope my column can do justice to the experience of Ralph's Italian Restaurant—a genuine piece of the history of our fair city. Tanti auguri!! Pax."

From Cleveland, Ohio, **Elaine Blanchard** writes, "While attending conferences in Philadelphia, I have enjoyed dining at your restaurant. Ralph's is the best in the world! I wish that you could send me a meal over the internet!!!

## Quotable . . .

". . . In restaurant land—where dining spots change hands almost as often as they do menus, and chefs make their reputations by creating the newest, trendiest, most startlingly inventive dishes— Ralph's is proud to be an antique . . . The dishes on the menu are the same ones that founder Francesco Dispigno and his wife, Catherine, served in 1900 to the working class men and women of their South Philadelphia neighborhood . . . God forbid some hotshot young chef should get any ideas about updating these classics or creating the kind of eclectic menu that's all the rage today . . . Brothers Jimmy and Eddie Rubino, Francesco's Great grandsons, claim they can tell if anyone so much as adds a new herb or spice to the tomato sauce . . . 'my Grandfather would roll over in his grave if we changed the menu,' said Jimmy . . . he will not let any dish leave the kitchen that is not true to the Ralph's tradition . . ."

Betty Cichy, The Bucks County Courier Times, March 22, 2000.

Yogi Berra, Michael Dispigno, Bob Dodaro and Gene Tenace.

# THE AFTERWORD . . .

A famous writer once wrote, "what's past is prologue," and in the case of Ralph's, that is certainly true. One hundred years after Francesco Dispigno's vision created Ralph's, his Great-Grandson Jimmy Rubino Jr. has a vision that will carry the restaurant and its name in to the 21$^{st}$ Century.

Last Spring, a new corporation was formed to carry the Ralph's tradition outside of Philadelphia. To avoid confusion with the original, the new restaurants will be known as "Jimmy Rubino's Ralph's of South Philadelphia".

The new organization is composed of Rubino as President and CEO, his brother Eddie as Chief Operating Officer, Ron Trombino as Vice President for Operations, William Lawson Esq. as general counsel, and this writer as Vice President for Sales and Marketing.

Leigh Donideau, editor of Cuizine Magazine, described Ralph's recently as ". . . a symbol, if not a temple, to the glory and joys of traditional Italian hospitality for 100 years . . ."

As Ralph's moves into the 21$^{st}$ Century, it will be our goal to carry Francesco and Ralph Dispigno's "temple of Italian hospitality" to the nation and, perhaps, the world.

The first 100 years were just the beginning. . . .

—Ted Taylor

# RALPH'S RESTAURANT AWARDS

## 'BEST OF PHILLY'
Philadelphia Magazine

1987, 1988, 1991,
1993, 1996,
1999

## 'READERS CHOICE AWARD'
*The City Paper*

1989, 1992, 1993
1994, 1995, 1996
1997, 1998, 1999

Voted One of Philly's "Top 3"
Restaurants in the last 25 Years by
"City Paper" readers in 1999

In addition to these awards,
we have consistently been given high ratings by
*Zagat's Restaurant Guide*

# BIBLIOGRAPHY & CREDITS

The authors wish to thank the following

Al Martino
Ann Malara
Anthony Barone
Anthony Pettino
Betty Cichy
Bob & Elaine Dodaro
Brett Taylor
Bucks County Courier Times
Chestnut Hill Local Newspaper
Christopher & Sue Taylor
The City Paper
Cynthia Taylor
*Departing Glory* by Joseph Gardner
Edward Rubino
Eleanor Montella
Fior d'Italia of San Francisco
Frank Quattrone
James Darren
Jennifer Kramer Williams
Joe Shay
John Corr
John Paoloca
Julie Duffy
Larry Howarth
Leigh Donideau
Len Lear

Michael Klein
Montgomery Newspapers
Pat Cooper
Philadelphia Daily News
Philadelphia Inquirer
Philadelphia Magazine
Phyllis Stein-Novak
Ralph Dispigno Jr.
Research-On-Demand, Berkeley, CA.
Restaurant Marketing Magazine
Ron Trombino
*South Philadelphia* by Murray Dubin
South Philadelphia Review & Chronicle
Stu Bykofsky
*The Cooking of Italy* by Waverly Root
The Food Network
The Theodore Roosevelt Society
Top Guns Corporate Photography
Vincent Schiavelli
William Lawson, Esq.
Xlibris
Zagat's Restaurant Survey

And to Francesco and Catherine Dispigno
for starting Ralph's in the first place . . .

# THE RECIPE FINDER...

# THE PEOPLE FINDER...

# ABOUT THE AUTHORS...

## JIMMY RUBINO JR.

A native of South Philadelphia, Jimmy grew up in Ralph's Restaurant and "worked" there from the age of six on. He always said that the restaurant was his "destiny." After graduating from South Philadelphia High School, he devoted all his energy to the restaurant, and at age 20—in 1981—Jimmy assumed the leadership role that has energized Ralph's and made sure that the family tradition would carry in to the 21st Century. Rubino's skills as a chef and his engaging personality have been widely quoted and recognized in the news media and he is a frequent guest on radio and TV. Rubino was one of the nation's leading Michael Jordan memorabilia collectors and now has compiled an impressive collection of corkscrews. Jimmy and his wife Holly have two children—Ryan and Gabrielle—and reside in suburban Bucks County, PA.

Jimmy Rubino, Jr.

# TED TAYLOR

"I am Italian by marriage, and that qualified me to work with Jimmy on this book." says Taylor of his 32-year-long union with the former Cynthia Mary DeMarco of South Philadelphia. President of his own Public Relations and Marketing firm, Taylor joined Ralph's as their publicist in 1999 and has worked with the restaurant on their year-long 100th anniversary celebration. Ted grew up in suburban Glenside and has been a baseball fan his entire life. (The fact that both he and Rubino collected sports memorabilia is what brought them together in the first place. They are friends first—the business thing came later on.) An educator by profession (he has been a college athletic director, baseball coach, and an English and Mass Media professor), Taylor has written two books on baseball card collecting and has been a sports hobby columnist for *The Philadelphia Daily News* since 1991. Ted and Cindy live in suburban Philadelphia and have four children and four grandchildren.

Ted Taylor